Milking the Haggis

(NEW WRITING SCOTLAND 21)

Edited by

VALERIE THORNTON
and
HAMISH WHYTE

with Maoilios Caimbeul (Gaelic Adviser)

Association for Scottish Literary Studies

Association for Scottish Literary Studies
c/o Department of Scottish History, 9 University Gardens
University of Glasgow, Glasgow G12 8QH
www.asls.org.uk

First published 2004

British Library Cataloguing in Publication Data

A CIP record for this book is available
from the British Library

ISBN 0–948877–57–X

The Association for Scottish Literary Studies
acknowledges the support of the Scottish Arts Council
towards the publication of this book

Typeset by Roger Booth Associates, Hassocks, West Sussex

Printed by Bell & Bain Ltd, Glasgow

CONTENTS

4

INTRODUCTION

Welcome – *New Writing Scotland* comes of age with its 21st birthday!

We had over 1100 submissions, from nearly 400 writers, and have had fun selecting 71 pieces from 52 writers.

We were encouraged by the range of writing that emerged and the sheer originality of much of it. We have humorous paeans to carrots and to shell-suits; we have a surreal heron, a leg-fetishist, stigmata, cannibalism and cold-blooded brutality; we have dry humour, gentle psychological probing, and deep compassion for outsiders from other countries or with other mentalities or on the other side of life; we have mainland writing and writing from over the water, from both the Western Isles and from the Northern Isles; by contrast, we also have work inspired by distant Lagos; we have writing that places a powerful emphasis on our sense of hearing; and we have chosen the title, Milking the Haggis, because it encapsulates the intriguing unexpectedness, combined with a sense of Scottishness, that characterises the essence of this anthology.

Astute regular readers may have noticed that the contents of at least 14 of the previous twenty NWS volumes have been arranged alphabetically by author. As we are the two most end-of-the-alphabet editors yet, we might like to redress this imbalance on behalf of our alphabetically-challenged fellows – watch this space!

We hope you enjoy this collection and if you were unlucky enough not to be selected for this issue, please don't be put off from submitting to *NWS* 22. As you can see, competition is fierce, and the standard of much that we could not include was also very high.

We look forward to reading your work and hope you enjoy reading our choices here.

Valerie Thornton
Hamish Whyte

NEW WRITING SCOTLAND 22

The twenty-second volume of *New Writing Scotland* will be published in summer 2005. Submissions are invited from writers resident in Scotland or Scots by birth or upbringing. Poetry, drama, short fiction or other creative prose may be submitted but not full-length plays or novels, though self-contained extracts are acceptable. The work must be neither previously published nor accepted for publication and may be in any of the languages of Scotland.

Submissions should be typed, double-spaced, on one side of the paper only and the sheets secured at the top-left corner. Prose pieces should carry an approximate word-count. **You should provide a covering letter, clearly marked with your name and address. Please do <u>not</u> put your name or other details on the individual works.** If you would like to receive an acknowledgement of receipt of your manuscript, please enclose a stamped addressed postcard. If you would like to be informed if your submission is unsuccessful, or if you would like your submissions returned, you should enclose a stamped addressed envelope with sufficient postage. Submissions should be sent by **30 September 2004**, in an A4 envelope marked for my attention, to the address below. We are sorry but we cannot accept submissions by fax or e-mail.

Please be aware that we have limited space in each edition, and therefore shorter pieces are more suitable – although longer items of exceptional quality may still be included. A maximum length of 3,500 words is suggested. Please send no more than two short stories and no more than six poems.

Duncan Jones
Managing Editor, *New Writing Scotland*
ASLS
c/o Department of Scottish History
9 University Gardens
University of Glasgow
Glasgow G12 8QH, Scotland
Tel: +44 (0)141 330 5309

James Aitchison

HOME TRUTHS

Walls Have Ears
'Walls Have Ears,' the war-time poster warned.
Indoors, our walls were bare but were adorned
with love and care and the ordinary cries
of children. No. This isn't an exercise
in nostalgia: my two-room childhood home
was bulldozed fifty years ago, a slum.

Two rooms, a fireplace, one cold-water tap.
And German spies immured there to entrap
us? Or were they walled in our backyard
communal lavatory? We had to guard
our words and sometimes keep our mouths
shut because the plain war-time home truths –
ours was a common Scottish family
home – could have comforted an enemy.

Foraging
You checked your gas mask in its cardboard box,
counted the coupons in our ration books
and then went tracking rumour from shop to shop.
McAndrew's? Just a row of meatless hooks
and sawdust without bloodstains. No fresh fruit
in Campbell's: 'The hail aipple/pear/plum crop
went to the Forces. Turnip, hen? Beetroot?'

Some days you reached the end of your pursuit.
In overall coats that hadn't been cut from jute
sacks but had a starch-fresh pre-war look,
women sliced cheese with wire in the Co-op,
pat-patted butter into half-pound blocks
and stacked small bars of pink carbolic soap.
Foraging is a force older than hope.

Death...
You vomited blood again, and were discharged
unfit for service in the Engineers
or any regiment. When you emerged
from hospital on your diet of steamed fish,
porridge and milk, you might have thought you'd years
and years ahead of you. And then your wish
for us – a new house, garden, and a lease
that's ours – came true! Beyond the boundary
fence, a burn's clear waterflow, a peace
of open fields, skylarks and a wide sky
on the horizon. But the strong new growth
you felt was cancer spreading through your brain
like god in his old role as psychopath.
At Easter-time you were released from pain.

...And Transfiguration
I was too terrified to join the men
who lowered your coffin into earth that day
in 1948 when I was ten
years old. And I'm still trying to repay
the debt. Perhaps my years of fearfulness
were just a version of the normal ills
of growing up, but I felt fatherless,
unfathered by your early death, until...?

There was no sudden change, no leap of faith;
time transformed you to your transmundane
yet natural condition of life-in-death:
arrays of living networks in my brain.

You sit up, smile, alive on your deathbed
like a forgiving god inside my head.

Liam Murray Bell

THE FIRST DAY OF CHRISTMAS

I don't get out much. In fact I never really leave my room. My mum lets me come downstairs three times a day for meals – breakfast, lunch and dinner – and I occasionally get to sit downstairs if we have visitors. Generally though, my parents are too ashamed to show me to the public. Still, I'm lucky in some respects. My parents' guilt at rearing a social recluse as a son has developed to such an acute paranoia of making me depressed that they buy me more or less anything I want. As a result I have a pretty sweet set-up in my room. The plasma screen television keeps me partially entertained with its incessant chatter, in surround sound, and blaring colour across its 22-inch flat screen. The rest of the time I spend on my state-of-the-art computer, surfing the world-wide web and talking to people from across the globe. The pool table in the centre of the room usually sits empty. Occasionally my dad deigns to play me at pool and when he does he furiously concentrates on getting the game over with as soon as possible, with the least possible interaction with me. Generally my parents keep out of the way though. There's one feature of the room that I love above all else, not a material possession. Indeed it's not even inside the room – it's outside.

I have a huge tree outside my window. It's a fruit tree that has boughs that stretch right across to the house next door. I like to look at it, to imagine myself spreading my branches like the wonderful, old, magnificent tree. I watch the leaves fall off in autumn and grow again in the springtime, I marvel at the re-birth. Maybe it's because I don't get out much, but that tree really fascinates me. I've come to think of it as my friend, my only friend.

I've never been to school – maybe my parents were too ashamed to enrol me. So I've learnt from home, studying textbooks, visiting websites, listening to tapes and watching educational programmes on my television. This method of learning has many advantages. I've discovered the joys of music – Verdi and Beethoven are my favourites – I've learnt how to touch-type, and studied the greatest philosophers of our time. I could accurately recount the entire history of the lead-up to both World Wars, and tell you of events during them. I've enjoyed reading all the great literary works of our age, and analysing their message. I could tell you exactly what Karl Marx believed and also tell you of the arguments against such an ideology. I can tell the difference between who and whom, and tell you how to make the perfect soufflé. I can speak in three different languages – but I think you get the point. Being stuck between four walls makes you want to learn – if only to relieve the monotony. I'm not writing this to brag though; I have a tale to tell.

At the beginning of November I turned seventeen. This was not momentous in any way, yet it did accompany one other, hugely significant, event. During the first week of November we got new neighbours. They moved in on a Saturday, the Thursday before had been my birthday – although when you're a prisoner in your own room every day feels basically the same. The long, tedious hours merge into each other and, as time passes, the days also begin to merge into one another, until it gets to the stage where I can't remember if I last spoke to a human being, other than my parents, two weeks or three weeks ago. Anyway, I digress. We got new neighbours. This event would not have changed the course of the day unduly if I hadn't happened to glance out of the window when the new neighbours arrived. They arrived in a big, black saloon car. There was a middle-aged couple in the front, who got out once the car had pulled to a stop. The man was fat and balding, with a grotesque goatee moustache that looked greasy, even from my view way up at my window. The woman was lavishly adorned in a suit that looked very expensive, although it was more than likely a clever fake of an expensive designer one. She looked like the kind to wear an entire bottle of perfume on top of her caked make-up, and possibly another bottle behind the ears – just in case anyone happened to venture there. The couple were unremarkable, and I was just about to turn away from the window when one of the back doors to the car started to open. I don't know what made me continue looking out of that window – something about the glint of blond hair transfixed my gaze. It was well worth staying for though. A tall, thin girl unfolded herself from the car and seemed to glide after the man and the woman, presumably her parents. She was captivating. There was something about her that drew my eyes towards her, something about her poise and appearance that made, previously alien, emotions stir within me. She had shoulder length golden hair that shimmered and shone in the sunlight. Even from my distant perch I could see the cornflower blue of her eyes and the sweetness of her smile. My heart fluttered as she threw a glance at my window. She hesitated and paused in the middle of one of her confident strides. Our eyes met through the grimy glass. She smiled. She actually smiled. Not many girls do that to me, although occasionally I get patronisingly pitying smiles from my rare visitors. She was the first person to meet and hold my gaze for many a year; even my mother had to look ashamedly away. The girl's smile had been sweet and genuine though, seemingly sincere in smiling at me through the window of my imprisoning room. I dreamt that night of sunsets and sunrises, of moonshine and starlight – I dreamt of the girl next door.

I asked my mother about the new neighbours at breakfast, subtly, though I needn't have bothered to be subtle since she didn't really pay much attention to me in any case. She said she'd met them the night before and that she'd taken them over some wine and welcomed them to the neighbourhood. The girl's name was Emma. Emma Partridge – what a divine name. I got lost in a vision of Emma Partridge and her cornflower blue eyes. My mother continued. She said they'd asked if I would like to show Emma round the neighbourhood since she was new here and we were the same age. My heart leapt – briefly. My mother had declined. She'd said – 'He doesn't get out much.' My mother had snubbed the girl of my dreams on my behalf – probably thought she'd be as embarrassed to be seen with me as my mum is. She probably would have been as well, most people were. My mother gave me her email address though, said I should talk to her online, welcome her to the neighbourhood. She always talks to me like I'm a cat or a dog, not a person. She's says it's just because I'm different, she says I have different needs.

That night I talked to Emma for the first time. I stayed up all night talking to her; she was just as perfect as I'd known she would be. We talked about books and animals and films. She liked Socrates and Freud, and she enjoyed Verdi, and although she didn't much care for Beethoven it was only a minor imperfection. She enjoyed painting and reading. She made me laugh with her stories of the outside world – of the world I never see except through a television screen or my grimy window. She was as captivating as she looked, and she didn't seem embarrassed to be speaking to me – though, I thought, that might well change. We talked about everything under the sun – until the sun rose to greet a new day.

I talked to her online every night after that – never stuck for anything to type as we chatted continually. After a few nights she asked me a question that made my heart leap and plummet in quick succession. 'Would you like to come over?' flashed the text on my screen. I paused for a moment before replying. 'I can't.' 'Why not?' came the reply. 'Mum wouldn't let me.' 'Oh.' The next message was from her as well, arriving too quickly for me to reply in the interim. 'Can I come over and see you?' she asked. 'Don't think my mum would let you.' I replied. Again the answer was 'Oh.' After that we didn't talk much, she sent 'Goodnight' and then logged off. She was gone forever, just like most people I talked to online. They didn't want to know me, who would? I lay and wept that night, with every lamentable love poem that I had ever read rushing through my head. She would never talk to me again – nobody ever did speak to me in person, only online; maybe they were too ashamed – like my mum. I lay on my back, unable to move, as the tears ran in rivulets down my face, and the snow started to drift down from the sky. The snow got heavier as my tears became waterfalls, and it was practically a blizzard as my tears changed into rivers. The snow was timely, though it made little difference to my broken heart, as the next day was the first day of Christmas. My advent calendar lay ready for me beside my bed, waiting for me to open the tiny windows. It was one of the highlights of my year, but then again, I don't get out much.

I awoke late the next day due to an interminable night spent mostly as an insomniac, a night spent weeping in my bed. The birds chirruped outside the window, anxious that I should wake up and herald the new day. What was the point though, every day was the same. Although today I was broken hearted. The snow lay heavy on the ground outside, deep and thick for the first day of Christmas. I'd never felt snow in my life – I didn't get out much. I moved over and began the arduous process of dressing myself on my own. I think every task, however menial, is made harder by a heavy heart. I didn't need to call my mother – I could manage without her. Then I opened the first tiny door on my advent calendar. It would certainly be the highlight of another long, boring, banal day. As I did so I closed my eyes and fervently wished. I really wanted this wish to come true. Christmas wishes seem like every other futile hope and prayer. I don't believe in miracles nor have any real religious faith as a rule, yet the desperate man turns to prayer, and I was desperate. So I prayed and I wished upon that first tiny flap of cardboard. I sat for what seemed like hours; my face screwed up into a wrinkled mass of skin behind my glasses. It was my one and only Christmas wish. I crossed my fingers and my toes, as far as was possible. Then I opened my eyes. I don't know what I expected, but I certainly didn't expect what I got. My wish had been granted. Sometimes fate smiles even on me, although my mum always said that I must have a lot of bad luck to have ended up as I am. My face broke into a smile as I moved slowly over to the window. My wish, my one and only prayer, had been answered. Outside, on the great boughs of my tree sat Emma Partridge, with a huge smile upon her face, and her cornflower blue eyes twinkling at me through the grimy window. I opened the latch and she scrambled in at the window and sat down beside me. She took my hand in hers and softly said, 'I decided that I would come and see you, no matter what your mother has to say about it.'

I'm still with Emma to this day; she still visits me by climbing across the tree. We're very much in love. The other day she even convinced my mum to let her push my wheelchair into town. She wheeled me through the park, through the pigeons and the children playing. I didn't feel in the least conspicuous with her. She wasn't always drawing attention to me, as my mother did with her unwanted fussing – not that she ever troubled to take me out. Emma was different though; she walked slowly and talked to me, pushing my wheelchair in front of her as if it were a pleasure rather than a chore. She didn't seem in the least bit ashamed and I was inordinately proud. We have wonderful plans for the future, and I can already see the boughs of my great tree beginning to stretch further and chart previously unseen terrain. Emma has opened my grimy window upon the world, and I can see the possibilities of spreading my branches, like my great friend the fruit tree. The magnificent tree had something to do with my happiness, as did a Christmas miracle. I'll always be grateful for my Christmas wish being granted. When, on the first day of Christmas, I looked out and saw Emma Partridge in my pear tree.

Neil Cocker

MILKING THE HAGGIS

Cammy opened the freezer. Growths of ice clung to the sides of the plastic chamber, fungus-like and two inches thick. Boxes of Estonian fishfingers were stacked on one side and a misted bottle of vodka on the other. In the back corner sat the haggis. He groped at it, a slippery cannonball frozen stuck like it had been welded to the plastic. He took out the fishfingers and vodka and stood them on the kitchen table out of harm's way. Cracked his knuckles. Then he got a good grip of the haggis with both hands, braced himself, and tugged.

The haggis jolted free, showering ice sparks onto the lino floor. He took it to the sink and rinsed off the permafrost. The running water streaked the haggis brown, revealing its pebble-dash insides, the lumps and grains of offal and oatmeal showing through its opaque skin. As he placed it on the worktop it clunked against the formica.

He put the haggis into the tupperware box and dropped it into his rucksack. The freezer door yawned open, and dry ice crept out, caught in the weak sunlight. He chucked the fishfingers back in and was about to put the vodka back too when he decided it would be a good time for a nip. It was Burns Day after all. He poured an inch into his Falkirk FC mug and knocked it back. Liquid ice, glowing lava. He spluttered, half-cough, half-laugh, and banged the mug back down on the worktop. Today would be alright, he decided. A chance to turn the corner.

On the walk to school snow fell like ash, clogging his hair and repatterning his puffa jacket. He could feel the weight of the haggis in his bag. As the school came into view a few kids ran past, rucksacks bouncing on their backs, feet kicking up slush. A snowball whizzed past his ear and impacted on the road, bursting into shrapnel. The vodka buzz was dying.

He went through the door and up the stairs, the corridors echoing with voices and the drumroll of running feet on the wooden floors. He had ten minutes to get ready. Ten minutes to draw a haggis and get his story straight.

His classroom was empty. He took a moment to compose himself and gazed up to the back wall, where the portraits of the Approved Writers hung. Hemingway, Burns, Byron,

Wordsworth, Faulkner, Dickens, Shakespeare. Most of them looked away, ashamed, embarrassed at some of things they had seen in this classroom. But Hemingway glowered at him as always, head poking out of his turtleneck sweater. His raging gaze seemed even more spiteful today.

Cammy wiped the board clean and got to work on his haggis drawing. The brittle chalk squeaked against the blackboard. He was nearly finished when the first kids came in, early morning blues clouding their expressions. The bell rang and the rest of 12A trooped in, including Jola, mouth full of bubble-gum. The ones who were talking stopped when they saw what was on the board.

Cammy pointed, a bit speechless himself. What was he doing with his life? Drawing fictitious animals in front of twenty teenagers in a concrete ghost town in the former Soviet Union? He cleared his throat and pointed again to the board.

They stared at his drawing.

His sketch showed the cliched, fool-the-sassenach blueprint of a beast with six legs (one side longer than the other), a bagpipes-shaped body, and a mosquito-like proboscis.

One of the kids in the front row put his hand up.

– Teacher... what is this?

Cammy rocked back and forward on his feet. – Can you guess?

– Elephant!

– Mosquito!

– Your girlfriend! said Jola.

He decided to ignore the girlfriend comment. – No. All wrong. It's a Scottish animal.

More perplexed faces.

He tossed his chalk in the air and caught it. – This is my drawing of the haggis. This animal lives in the mountains of Scotland. It feeds on the blood of American tourists. It is a stupid animal though. It walks in circles around the mountains until it gets so dizzy it loses its balance and falls to its death. The Scots go to the bottom of the mountains, scrape up what's left of the haggis, put it in a plastic bag, and cook it.

A room full of teenagers, staring at him in disbelief. He opened his rucksack and took out the tupperware box, and slowly peeled back the lid to reveal the haggis.

– Teacher, it's a joke!

– It's a joke! It's a joke!

– Okay… He gestured back at the blackboard. – This is what we tell Americans as a test to see how stupid they are.

12A laughed. They obviously liked the concept of making Americans look stupid.

– Do you want to know the truth?

– Yes, said one of the kids, deadly serious. – Please teacher. We need the truth.

– This is a food we eat on a special day of the year. The birthday of Robert Burns. Scotland's national poet.

He pointed up at the picture of Burns. The kids turned to the back of the room.

– He is very angry, said one of them.

– No, said Cammy. – That's Hemingway. Robert Burns is next to him.

A flat pop sounded from the front row. Cammy glanced over to see Jola with a membrane of gum stuck to her lips. She peeled it back into her mouth and started her slow chew again.

Cammy paused. Then continued. – Burns was passionate about many things. Human rights, alcohol…

– Just like Cammy, said Jola.

He opened his mouth to speak but was interrupted by a wail from outside. He sat on his desk and waited. All of them waited. The nuclear siren droned its banshee whine, lifting the crows from the trees outside, its screech rising and vibrating the windows. Cammy bit his lip and stared at his feet. After thirty seconds or so it tailed off, shuddering, its dying lament drooping away. Cammy watched the kids as they sat and looked into space, puddle-eyed.

Then there was silence. Cammy stood up again. – This nuclear siren goes off once a month. I am told it's practice. How would you know if it was for real?

There was a pause as they digested his question. Then Jola put her hand up.

– We do not know if it is real or not. It means nothing. If there was a problem with the nuclear station in Jonava…

– Yes?

– Well, we would probably be dead a few hours after hearing the cry. What could we do?

– So why the siren?

Jola smiled at him. – It lets us know how long we have left.

Cammy put his hand in the tupperware box and closed his fingers around the haggis. Still cold, a defrosting shotputt. He knew the kids were watching him. He picked up the haggis and held it above his head.

– Do you want to come with me to the school kitchens and cook this?

They looked at him, uncertain.

And as he stood with the blood draining from his arm, half-frozen haggis suspended above him, he imagined the power station at Jonava melting down, tendrils of nuclear mist creeping across the snowfields, radiation sifting into the air and poisoning the breeze. An invisible death blowing towards them.

– Okay, said Jola. – Let's go cook this haggis.

Linda Cracknell

STILL BY THE POOL

In the row of six still silent children, she's the one who reaches out to press the button, re-charging the shower when the flow gasps and stops. The hot water glosses her head seal-like, falls in splashes around her thin veined feet. She stares out across the stilling swimming-pool. It's empty except for the red float that spins to remind the afternoon of plunging laughter. Her swimming costume clings pink, and between her shoulders, the whisper of a shiver. A figure in marble waiting for a signal.

> I've never seen.
> So still.
> So blue.
> Why blue?
> I've never seen.
> His face.
> Did you see?
> And his mum crouched over him.
> With his feet still in the water.
> The other lady kissing with life.
> But he's already.
> Isn't he?
> Blue.
> His mum crying, hands over mouth.
> And if he.
> Squeeze eyes shut.
> Wish two minutes back.
> Can we?
> Please god.
> We were splash-happy.
> Mum.
> I wish you were here.
> Smiling, not crying.
> His red float, still circling, turtle-shaped.
> He was a frog with leaping legs.
> Splash-happy.
> Two minutes ago.

David Cunningham

STOP OUT

I stood in a corner of the club, hating it. The air was hazy and raked by pencil-thin beams of light. The implacable throb of the music made me feel as if I were trapped inside a toothache. I was only here because I'd recently broken up with my girl-friend and my flatmates had decided that I needed 'cheering up'. Too enfeebled by melancholy to resist, I'd gone along with their plans for my first Saturday night out as a single man in five years.

A female figure approached around the pulsating fringe of the dance floor. She held two bottles of beer above her head. Her name was Siobhan – a friend of the girlfriend of one of my flatmates. She handed me my beer and clinked hers against it, causing a thin stream of bubbles to issue from its neck.

'Thanks,' I yelled.

'Enjoying yourself, Gregor?' she yelled back.

I nodded wanly. She sported an array of ironmongery: ring through the lip, stud in the nose, another ring through the right eyebrow. It looked incongruous, even vaguely barbaric, set against her guileless, freckled features. Nonetheless the slight curve of her belly, between the hem of her cropped T-shirt and the top of her hipster jeans, was sweetly sexy.

'While since you've been to a club?' she yelled.

'Isobel was never a great clubber.'

'Were you?'

'What?'

'Were *you*?'

'Well, I like a dance now and then. But it's a bit loud for me.'

'What?'

'I said it's a bit loud for me.'

'Sorry I can't hear you, it's too loud. Come a bit closer.'

Of course. I'd forgotten the protocol for holding a conver-sation in a club: you place your lips about an inch from your interlocutor's ear and yell something; you turn your head; she places her lips about an inch from your ear and yells something back; she turns her head and on it goes. During an especially heated exchange the pair of you look as if you've just emerged from a cuckoo clock.

'When we were students we were both skint,' I explained. 'So we didn't really go out much at all. We used to cook together a lot. We'd find cheap recipes to try out. Then we'd usually play Scrabble. Sometimes we'd read to each other as well or watch an old film.'

I noticed the bemused expression stealing across her face as she gazed at the floor, head tilted towards me.

'And then, at the end of the night, we'd both put our teeth in a glass of water and go to bed,' I finished, with a self-conscious laugh.

She turned her head and smiled. Though I'd only met her a couple of times before, I knew her to be smart and articulate. But when she was out she seemed to adopt the persona of the constantly distracted professional clubber, most comfortable with small talk. Then again, perhaps she was on something. If she was I'd be the last person to realise.

'Well, you can have some fun now, eh?' she said. 'I'll be back in a minute.'

Alone again in the pounding darkness, I found my thoughts turning to Isobel. They never left her for long these days. The idea of her seemed to exert a far stronger pull than it ever had when we were together.

I suppose we *were* a fogeyish kind of couple. We'd met as first year undergraduates. We'd both had unprecocious island childhoods, roaming under limitless skies. We'd both lost a parent in our mid-teens. We were both virgins. When we started going out together everything had – as people euphemistically put it – 'fallen into place'. Reticent in most other respects, Isobel was unembarrassed about showing me what she wanted. As clueless as any young man, but perhaps less concerned than most with pretending I knew it all, I was grateful to be shown. Meanwhile, all around us, the hormonal stew of university life bubbled away. As we looked on, somewhat daunted, our friends got drunk, slept around, suffered the after-effects of dodgy pills, made supplicatory Sunday morning visits to the family planning clinic. Our bed seemed to be a still centre. Usually in it before midnight, we counted ourselves blessed to have found one another and avoided all those other convulsions that looked like such a strain on the nervous system.

Siobhan was back, looking considerably more alert and wielding another two bottles of beer. She gestured to indicate that she wanted to say something.

'So what happened?' she asked.

'When?'

'With you and Isobel.'

'Oh... I don't know. After we graduated she wanted to go back to Mull to be near her folks. She never really liked city life. But I already had a job here. And I suppose things had started to cool off a little bit. Then she went to Aberdeen to do a post-grad in librarianship at Robert Gordon's. So we only saw each other at the weekend. Then, after a while, it was every second weekend. I think maybe if you have to travel to see each other it becomes much more obvious that the energy is leaking out of a relationship.'

'Was there anyone else?'

'Not as far as I know.'

Shouting loudly about things you would normally talk about – if at all – in a hushed monotone was an odd and unsettling experience. I lapsed into a brooding silence. No, there wasn't anyone else. But there was, on my side and, I suspect, on hers the *idea* of someone else. It's the classic pattern of a youthful relationship: passion for one another fades but passion itself remains coarsely robust. Grief at the failure of love might diminish it for a while, but it will soon reassert itself. Had Isobel and I been together fifty years earlier, passion's end would have meant a passionless life together from then on. Now though, fogeyish as we were, we believed like everyone else that our individual happiness was the supreme consideration.

Siobhan was staring at me. I could tell that all sorts of calculations were being carried out inside her head: desire divided by practicality, multiplied by expedience. Apparently reaching a conclusion, she curled her fingers round the back of my neck and drew me towards her. My mouth opened obligingly in surprise.

*

We fell into Siobhan's room and, because the room was so small, straight on to the bed. As we began to undress one another the light from the street lamp bleached our already pale northern flesh. Fingers gloved by drink, we struggled with buttons and zips.

It soon became clear, however, that something wasn't right. The tocsin of moans and grunts we emitted to persuade one another (and ourselves) that we were comfortable in this situation couldn't hold at bay the sense of unreality that was creeping over me. All the grappling seemed to have disconnected some vital wire that connected the sensations of pleasure to my animal parts. The instant I realised this, of course, I embarked on a downward spiral of anxiety from which there was little chance of return. Like countless men before me, I blustered on regardless.

Fairly soon, however, Siobhan's writhing became more and more perfunctory, then stopped altogether. With a resigned sigh she turned away from me. Clinging to the edge of the bed, contemplating her hunched back, I felt like a comedian who, having failed to make the audience laugh, remains stranded on the stage as they talk amongst themselves, pointedly ignoring him.

What was the accepted protocol for a situation like this? Did you slope off into the night or try to explain? The first option seemed preferable since I had no idea what the explanation was. On the other hand, I felt so drained by my fiasco that sloping anywhere was beyond me.

How little I really knew about modern mores. My years with Isobel had lulled me into imagining that I was a reasonably sensitive lover with a varied repertoire. But, where casual sex was concerned, all those things became superfluous next to the bluntly mechanical.

At last, Siobhan turned to me.

'I'm sorry,' I told her. There was nothing else I could say.

'It's all right,' she replied. Since there were all sorts of other things that *she* could have said, I was grateful that she said this.

'I've never done this before. I mean just met someone in a club and...'

'Uhuh.'

'I didn't imagine it would be so difficult. It's nothing to do with you, honestly.'

She favoured this with a tolerant but unamused smile.

'I didn't think it was actually.'

Turning away again, she rummaged in her handbag, which lay on the floor beside the bed.

'Not everyone's cut out for this kind of thing you know,' she continued. 'Oddly enough, I sometimes think women are much better designed for sleeping around than men, physically at any rate. We don't have to worry about brewer's droop. We can do it if we have to without feeling especially turned on because we can fake most of it. And where opportunity's concerned, well, most men are always gagging for it, or think they are anyway.

'But if you've been looking around thinking everyone else is having a great time shagging anything that moves, it isn't always the way it appears, you know. I mean, sometimes it is really good. But that's usually only if you're doing it with someone you'd like to have for more than just the night. And then of course you can't say anything because that would be really uncool.'

She hoisted herself upright again, a lit cigarette dangling between her lips.

'Believe me, I should know,' she added.

Pushing her hair out of her face, she waggled her toes, which protruded from the bottom of the duvet, and contemplated their chipped nail varnish.

'None of this ever occurred to me before,' I said.

'Well it wouldn't, would it? You've been cosily in a relationship since you were, what, ten? Women are getting less embarrassed these days about doing what they feel like. Quite right too, I say. But at the same time men are getting more sensitive – to themselves at any rate. They also know that all the magazines have taught women to expect a lot more in bed. So they start worrying about it. And the more they worry about it the greater the chance that they'll... come up short, so to speak. At least that's what happens to most of the ones who might be any good. The morons, who you wouldn't be interested in anyway, don't worry about it.

'It's the same crappy dilemma that women are always faced with. You can have the vote but only when it doesn't really mean anything anymore. You can have a career, but just when it's going well you'll have to panic about having kids before it's too late. You can behave like a man sexually, but only when men are starting to have problems behaving like men themselves.'

'Ouch.'

'Don't worry,' she said. 'There's nothing much wrong with you. This just isn't your kind of thing. Sometimes you have to try it to find out. But it makes it a bit... well, maybe hard's not the word. But it makes it a bit tough on the person you try it with.'

'But I do really fancy you,' I said, sounding as shrill and plaintive as a thirteen year old. 'Maybe if we spent some more time together, got to know each other a bit better...'

'But you don't really want to get to know me any better, do you?'

'Well...'

'It's okay. Stick to being a nice boyfriend and you'll be fine.'

'Seems to cut out a lot of options though.'

'Well, there's always Viagra I suppose.'

'Oh thanks very much.'

She doubled over laughing, the laugh eventually disintegrating into a cough. Patting her back, I felt a surge of gratitude towards her for teaching me so much so painlessly.

'You know...' I began.

'Now that I've given you such an easy time about this you like me much more.'

'Yes.'

'Yeah, I'm a real sexual Samaritan.'

'I've got a lot to learn, haven't I?'

'You certainly have. But in the meantime you can make me a cup of tea.'

'You mean I can stay?'

'Course you can stay. After all you never know. Things might look up in the morning.'

Mike Dillon

INSUFFERABLE ROMANTICS

I hate these insufferable romantics
walking around, hand in hand
slobbering over each other and
drowning in each other's eyes
blind to every wrinkle and grey hair
with never a thought of the disgust
engendered by the sight of their
Geriatric Fumblings.

I hate these insufferable romantics
with their half-apologies and aphorisms.
I think I'll scream the next time I hear
'It's better the seventh time round'
or 'You're only middle-aged once'.
Death's too good for the bastards,
pretending they're still eighteen
and boasting about their latest
attack of acne.

I hate these insufferable romantics
acting as if they'd found an emerald
in this world of middens and corruption.
They've just no consideration at all
inflicting their pathetic soppiness
on those who know how to act their age.
It really ought not to be allowed:
smiling into each other's souls
as if they finally knew the answer
to every question.

I hate these insufferable romantics
especially in the narrow nights
when the cold winds whisper
they might be right.

Angus Dunn

MANY LEGS

The millipede has not got a thousand legs. The centipede has
far less than a hundred. Only when we move further down the
scale of leggy multiplicity do we find that popular belief is close
to accurate. While the squid has most people baffled, it is both
widely and correctly believed that the octopus has eight legs.
And insects have six. Though here there is room for discussion,
if not outright contention: an insect's antennae are modified
legs and even its mandibles are legs that have developed into
strange but useful forms. We have all seen a close-up shot of an
ant or a beetle eating: it is using different motions, different
actions, even different organs from those that we use for the
task. Some of us find this oddness deeply disturbing.

Among humans, our legs rarely have anything to do with
our eating practices, though it has to be said that in cases of
enforced cannibalism – and presumably also in elective cannibalism – the leg is a prized portion, being fine and fleshy. And
most of us find this disturbing also.

An acquaintance of mine once felt compelled to show me
a very old encyclopaedia that he had obtained in an auction.
In this book was a monochrome photograph of a Russian
commissar sitting by a stout man with a thick peasant face.
They were on a bench outside; the ground was white with
snow and they both wore clothes of fur. The commissar looked
a little smarter but he wore his hat at an odd angle as if he was,
if not drunk, then a little tipsy.

I could see little of note in the picture, until I read the
caption. It appeared that in times of famine, the stout man
sold human flesh to the people of the area. It was a family
tradition. No-one else sold human meat, just this man and his
family. For several generations, they had occupied, and indeed
defended, this economic niche. There was no suggestion that
they killed people. Their trade was an opportunistic one: they
were scavengers rather than predators. Though it appeared
from the text that, in a bad year, it was a full-time occupation.

The commissar, who had evidently set up the photographic
session, did not look afraid or even worried, to be sitting next
to a purveyor of human meat. This was as disquieting as anything else – that this official seemed to find the situation a bit

of a lark, rather than deplorable. He might even carry a copy of the photo around in his wallet, to show to strangers in bars.

'Look, this is me, and this is the cannibal butcher of Rodinsk!'

Looking more closely at the picture, the background details became clearer. What appeared to be a pile of old clothes was, in fact, a human body, still clothed, lying on a heavy table. A leg was lying on the icy ground, in a macabre visual pun, beside the table leg. Other bits and several whole bodies were stacked against the wooden wall behind.

The picture was fascinating, though I suppose that it was my response that was most interesting. I looked at the picture and saw two men, quite normal-looking, though in an old-fashioned way. After I looked at the background, their faces changed, grew sinister.

Pictures of mass-murderers, politicians, habitual misusers of the possessive apostrophe and other similar human renegades, rarely show anything unusual. I might look at a photo in the newspapers and think that this person looks like any everyday person you might meet on the street. Then I read what the person did or is accused of, and the relaxed smile becomes a ruthless sneer. The calm gaze becomes the blank stare of a psychopath. That is understandable, of course. We project our thoughts and emotions onto other people. Given a set of photos of perfectly normal people mixed in with these criminals, I could not pick out any essential difference. On the visual evidence alone, these people are normal. And that is worrying. Could I be living next door to a mass-murderer? A cannibal? Conversely, the man across the road, who wears a neatly trimmed brown moustache and carries a meat cleaver in his belt – is he, in fact, perfectly normal?

When I was of an impressionable age, I read an essay of George Orwell's. In the course of his essay Orwell claimed that food rarely looks like food, though he does give just one counter-example. He comments on a species of antelope, saying that it was impossible to look at the hindquarters of the beast without thinking of mint sauce. The rest of his essay is lost to me, though I think it was about the use of words.

If we can project our emotions on to newspaper pictures of violent and degraded people, then plainly we can do the same for foods. I suspect that Orwell was not a gustatorily oriented person. Or perhaps he was rarely hungry. I have been hungry and I can tell you that a young cauliflower is an unalloyed delight, and on occasion I have nearly wept over a carrot.

To be fair to Orwell, I think he was referring specifically to animals. Yet even here, it seems to me that he betrays a lack of culinary imagination. I have experimented over the years, discovering that while it may have been true for Mr Orwell, it is by no means so for me. It is true that a dog, no matter how hard I try to imagine it, cannot look like food. Even the American hot dog does not look like food to me. Similarly with the cat. I think it is the hairiness that puts me off.

Cows rarely look like food – but I once met a water buffalo in India that seemed to invite the carving knife. It looked at me with its beautiful brown eyes and let me pat its shoulder. I had even been introduced to it and to its owner, but I could not help thinking what a fine meal it would make. Pigs too, especially the piglets, look very toothsome. Perhaps other people find the sheep a delectable mammal, but I do not. A lamb, yes, but not a full-grown sheep. I'm sure that there are personal preferences in these things.

Orwell's assertion remained with me, however. I was annoyed that I couldn't argue it out with him. Now and then I would check it out once more: yes, that mackerel still says, 'Eat me'; that rabbit is crying out to be served in a thick gravy with bay-leaves. And then I would tell myself, 'See? He was wrong.'

I encountered a girl called Jill. She had long dark hennaed hair and wore hippy skirts and a wonderful scent with a hint of citrus and vanilla. I was nervous of approaching her directly, but eventually, without too much engineering on my part, I found myself sharing a drink with her and several of our mutual friends. I was delighted to find that she noticed and seemed to reciprocate my interest. We chattered about nothing in particular and laughed at things that were not funny. Eyes looked into eyes – it was going pretty well. Then she had to visit the toilet, and as she slid out from the banquette seat, her skirt rode up and I saw her leg right up to her solid thigh. My heart gave a little leap and she smiled at me as I blushed and turned my head away.

I sat there, aware that I was a little drunk and might be misreading the situation. 'She was just embarrassed,' I told myself – but her smile had definitely held more than that. The brief flash of thigh drifted into my mind's eye – and as will happen to a lovesick person, it acquired all sorts of alluring properties.

I could feel myself melting. But I knew exactly what happened when I let myself melt. I became incapable of conversing rationally and I lost all practical ability to perform everyday actions like standing up without knocking over a chair or opening a door courteously without looking and feeling like a fool.

So I carefully, in a mature and sensible way, looked at my reaction to her thigh. It's just a thigh, I thought. Be sensible. What effect can a thigh have on you? You've got two of them, everyone has. The vision of her thigh drifted up in front of me, desire arose and before I could stop it, George Orwell's little throwaway comment drifted into my mind. Jill's thigh suddenly looked like the most wonderful food. I laughed the thought away. Amazing what the mind could do.

Jill returned and sat closer to me than before, so that her leg was touching mine. In a few short minutes, time was called and we all drifted out into the street. Jill and I dragged our feet, letting everyone walk further and further ahead of us. They all turned the corner and Jill took my hand and pulled me into a doorway. In a moment our lips were pressed against each other, mouths opening as we urgently tried to press them still closer.

When the thought arrived, I stopped moving completely, then shuddered. Jill held herself against me for a moment longer, then pulled away and looked up.

'You all right?'

'Yes. Sorry. I've got to get home.'

'What? What's wrong?'

'George Orwell,' I said. 'And the mandibles of insects.'

'Insects!'

'Not just insects,' I said, unhappily. 'Segmented beasts in general.'

I think, if people still did such things, she would have slapped my face. And I wouldn't have blamed her. In fact, it might have made me feel a bit better. Instead, she kicked me in the knee. It was very painful, and my leg collapsed.

I looked up at her, glaring down at me. 'Your legs are beautiful,' I said. And indeed they were – tall and solid legs that were both sensual and muscular. I lay there, my heart aching as I listened to her shoes clacking away up the street. She left behind her a sweet scent of citrus and vanilla.

Angus Dunn

MISPLACED

a black and white duckish bird
whirring
just above the waves
– a humming bird misplaced
amongst the gales and heavy waters
hopelessly seeking nectar
and finding nothing
but salt

STEALING

Why punish you with chains
and vultures?
The work is not easy or painless
even for one so strong.
But year after year
you keep at it,
learning. Slowly, but well.
'Don't clench it lad,
don't hold it tightly now, Prometheus,
but carry fire lightly, lightly.'

Alexis Ferguson

THE SIBLINGS IN THE CUPBOARD

Don't remember what age I was; young. Remember the feeling of being stung by the fact it was alive. I mean, used to be alive. Know I was young; one of those memories that grow with mental age, perception adds bits to memories, make it seem like yesterday. But young enough to investigate boxes without reading labels first. Old brown labels, faded and closetbrowned ink. So I picked up the other box first. Blue velvet, brass hasps. Inside; old film reel, old religiosity steeped artefacts; show up old feelings and superstitions of a time long past. Irrelevant, but still unspeakable. A mounted rock crystal. Palmsmooth. Behind it, old brown boxes. Tiny, by comparison. About the dimensions of a hand. It whispered. The other box; bigger. Full baby size, had I noticed. It rattled. Turned over: the bottom screwed shut. Four star-screws, slightly raised. The wood was old, rough, untreated since it was hewn, before I was born. Slightly less than nine months, had I noticed. I pulled, looking for a lid. Thwarted, I dumped them on the table, rested my chin on top. Felt, and remembered the label. This was my brother. Brother. I have. I had. I did have one. Brother. A brother! My Brother Duncan.

I had had a brother Duncan. His charred dust. I had picked him up and shaken him.

I had had a brother? His cremated baby dust? Moved to the bigger box.

A sister. Remains. Had rattled. I had jingled my sister Helen's bones. No cremation for her. Her dried remains. They could not rub her heart back to life.

It had lain, dried, in this darkness all my life while mine had squishied on, once it was made. Mine was moist and fat, it squelched and I could hear it, feel it, see it. The box is big. Why is she dry? Had they poked holes in her to see what's wrong? What was wrong? Why? She is not burned. 'Remains' it says.

Large baby box. Rattles. Is it just dust and bones? Can you make out the head? The feet? Such tiny, they must be! Locked in a screwed-shut box in the top of a cupboard. High place, not for babies. Why are they still here, is that normal? It will be dark in there. Dark and cold and dusty, for longer than I've been here. Not a good place for babies. Dangerous, to be so high. They wouldn't like it. Are they visited very often?

Dark and cold and dusty.
'Would you like some tea, dear?'
'No, thank you.'
'Have some milk then?'
Their grubby chubby hands, older than mine, dried and packed and burned. How would they even lift the teapot?

Stir in the arsenic, stir, stir, stirristirstir so it all goes in, or was it the holes poked in them? Before their nine months, perhaps? Impatient, to see the world spread out flat for the butcher's knife? The chloroform and plasma, drugs and tubes and anti-septic, all laid out on glittering black night-wine at dusk, with blood-red circles?

Impatient to leave, and see the next thing 'cause there has to be a next thing, right? The people no one knew, who knew no-one, who do they look for at that next place? His personality; a rough-cut box, with star screws.

Whispers if you shake him. Someone here called him Duncan once. Will my sister be angry I jangled her bones?

Alexis Ferguson

THE SPYING GAME

Today I think I'll kill something. I feel that way.
I'm fed up being ignored, and boredom
Shuffles forward with its hands up in the air.
Today I am God, and someone ought to know.

Someone whispers on the stair,
Muffled sounds of red and black,
Who whispers? What is there?
Noises unspoken, half drawn back?

I see ants on the ground, and fry them
With a magnifying glass.
They are a different language now, like Shakespeare.

Someone is padding up the stair,
Flitting as a shadow past all doorways,
Never standing a moment anywhere.

The dog avoids me. It knows I am a genius
And is ashamed of itself. It knows that today I am
Going to change the world, something's world.

Many whispers gather to open the door, wide,
You see: it is not true, they have lied.
Yet, words lie as heavy dust,
Infesting rooms, red bubbles on iron, as rust.

Who leaves them? Someone must.

I breathe out talent and fog the glass,
There is nothing left to kill.
I find the bread-knife and go outside.
The streetlights glitter, I tap your arm.

Rody Gorman

BEÀRNAN-BRÌDE / *DANDELION*

Rabhadh a bheireadh i fhìn seachad:
Na beanaibh ris a' Bheàrnan-Bhrìde!
'S cha b'e ruith ach leum leinn
Gus an rud fheuchainn.

> *She used to warn us:*
> *Don't go near those dandelions!*
> *and, of course,*
> *we could hardly wait to try them.*

An toiseach-gnothaich,
Bhiodh tu gad lùbadh fhèin
Gus a bhuain is ga thogail an àirde.
Bhriseadh tu 'n gas.

> *First of all, you bent down*
> *to pick it and get it up.*
> *Then, you broke off the stem.*

An uair sin, spreadhadh a' bhrìgh gheal na bhroinn às.
An uair sin, bhiodh tu ga chur na do chraos.
An uair sin, ga shluigeadh sìos
Agus, an uair sin,

Mus canadh tu seachd,
Bha thu air an gnothach a dhèanamh.

> *Then, all that sap*
> *inside it came spurting out.*
> *You put it in your mouth after that*
> *and swallowed it whole*
>
> *and then, before*
> *you could say Jack Robinson,*
> *you were done.*

Charlie Gracie

COMING OF AGE

'Where are you from?' you said to him, carefully, him being obviously foreign.

'Slovakia.'

'Ah, Bratislava,' you nodded, no clue where that had come from or anything – just out. Automatic. Instinctive.

'No. Kosice. In the east.' His dark eyes had a fullness to them like there was never going to be enough time to take it all in. Perhaps a touch forlorn, far from home, but full of expectation. Hope.

'I am looking-g for the youth hostel.' He swept his hand through the black hair which the rain had flattened against his head.

You knew it was going to be easy from there. You just had to insist that he come home to meet the family – you would get changed and drive him to the hostel. He could savour some Scottish hospitality. Your children would love to meet a Slovakian.

So here you are bumping up the dirt track like a hunter-gatherer, a Slovak in the passenger seat. Dragging him into the porch to meet the bright light and the wide eyes of your three children and the warm smile of your wife that you kiss

slowly

and the heat of the kitchen running out the door to meet you, the Slovak standing like a sheep in the porch squinting in the light and the brightness of your children and your wife. Not knowing what is coming next.

The smell. Wonderful from the kitchen. Lamb something, herby and fatty, the smell of fat and herbs and lamb mingling with the excited talk in the porch and the wee Slovak standing looking into the light.

In a flurry of jackets and boots, rucksack, sleeping mat, rain dripping all ways, the smell of Slovakian sweat mixing with Scottish sweat and a lamb dinner, you are all out of the outdoor things and into the kitchen, him standing on the tiled floor looking around the room, the photographs on the ochre walls the Aga with pots chirping away the huge table that can sit thirteen with ease the autumn's clutch of onions and garlic hanging in well formed bunches above it. He rubs his arms warmly and smiles at you all.

You go round the family one by one, introducing your wife, then the two boys,

'...my son Steven who is nine... Peter who is eight...'

And then Sara.

The children, their usual diffidence with a stranger. He with his hand outstretched to each in turn

'I am so very happy to make your acquaintance.....'

and he does a funny handshake to Steven and Peter, which makes them laugh and in a minute with the ice cracked, we are round the big table and the wine open and you suddenly remember something.

'Slovakian – beer! I've got some Slovakian beer somewhere' you scrabble about in the back of the cupboard for it. 'Here we are – Starapromen...'

'Czech,' he says with a simple – almost beautiful – smile, and your wife joshes you for it, and he lowers his head the way that boys do with a crush on their teacher and Sara does the 'DUHUH!' thing and the Slovak looks at her quizzically

and you can see that Sara has her eye on him.

This is the thing really. It's not just bringing a stranger into the house

to savour some Scottish hospitality

you're introducing something else into the dynamic. Tonight could have gone like this

sitting down after a lamb dinner
kissing your wife on the warm smile
coorying into the children coorying into you
music in the dark corner of the room
the smell of herbs and the taste of lamb
all greasy and tasty
in the hours into the night.

But here you are with a Slovak.

And a thirteen-year-old daughter with her eye on him.

And two boys who want to stalk him, skulking round the table, hungrily, smiling at the stranger, he smiling back, your wife telling them to sit at peace and wait.

'Wait for a bit, boys,' she whispers.

and everything else that will now inevitably follow

'Tell us, Filip,' – F i l i p he spelled it carefully, knowing that there was a different way, a British way, 'tell us, Filip, about Kosice.'

Potatoes pass around the table in the big dish.

Filip spoons some onto his plate, rolling them beside the lamb and the carrots. Wipes his hands on his trousers, looks at the space between the top of your heads and the ceiling as if he were trying to read the answer and says,

'Not so beautiful as Stirling-g.' Coy. 'Kosice is a little larger, without a castle, but we have our Andrassy Palace which is beautiful in the centre of the city.'

He leaves for a moment, then returns with a small daysack and fumbles a leather folder from inside it. He draws out a number of photographs and a brochure and places them one by one on the table.

He beams at the tiled roofs and crumbled walls of the town, and the smiling faces of his mother and brother and three younger sisters who are still at school and wear red dresses, and his brother works as a blacksmith with his uncle who has been like their father since he died when Filip was ten years old in the road with a car coming too fast around the corner, no-one seeing who was the driver and the town mourning as if their own father and husband and son it had been who had died. The flowers in big vats by the doorstep where his mother, younger and thinner than you might imagine, looks straight into the camera, straight out of the photograph into the kitchen where you sit listening to Filip tell the story of his family, of heat and work and the Velvet Revolution. The Andrassy Palace sits on the front of the brochure, neo-Baroque gargoyles leering from the corner turret, a family strolling among the gardened edge of it, strolling in the quiet sunshine across to the streets beyond.

'It's a very beautiful place,' your wife says, and Filip beams again.

'Thank you.' Sits back in the chair with the air of a man who has thrown down three aces and two kings. He puts a potato into his mouth and smiles round at you for a moment, then gathers the photographs together and shuffles them back into the leather folder.

'Would you like?' He hands the brochure to Sara, KOSICE emblazoned proudly across the front.

'Thank you,' and takes it onto her knee under the table, glancing through it. You are glad she is polite. It is always better to be polite.

BUT   You know that moment when you know that a moment has come?

Sara has always been an eager girl. You never really worry as such, but you are aware of it. It's a good thing of course. There is no denying it.

It's just the way she leaves the room. And Filip certainly notices.

She rises slowly.

'Thank you, Filip,' stretches out, yawns to the ceiling, arms just a little back like a swan in the second before lift off, onto her toes, chin up and back to the surface in a splashless touch of heel.

You look at her. You remember the first time you had to take care of a stranger yourself. You remember the fear and excitement mixing, your father egging you on, all the talking beforehand. But Sara did not need all that – she watched. Learned. Took things in quietly.

And she is the very girl to take it all on.

Sara exits with the brochure in hand, her first trophy it could be said.

The rest of you sit for a moment in the smell of lamb and buttered carrots

an almost imperceptible moment.

Nothing is said. Filip coughs and straightens in his chair, you in yours, your wife in hers – though you know that she is relaxed about all of this, more than you are that's for sure, and that you both have known that when Sara gets to a certain age she will stretch herself, make decisions, take moments when they arise, fill the space which you have tended for her all these years and fill it as big as you or your wife have filled yours.

Filip seems to shrink a bit. His space shrinks a bit.

Your two sons break the silence

BANG   BANG   YOU'RE DEAD

and everyone laughs. Even Filip.

And then Sara comes in
her moment
with a garden fork. She strides behind Filip, unseen by him
and thrusts the fork through the space in the chair into the
small of his back. She is a strong girl.

You think about her helping the neighbouring farmer with
the lambing, even at the age of ten wrestling yows to the grass
to let the farmer get a good look at them, happy to tangle on
the ground with the legs kicking out and the horns, no fear, the
yow bleating and writhing and Sara holding on not saying a
word just being in charge
so the fork sticks right in, and she gives the handle a twist
as it reaches its limit
a moment of nothing and Filip breaks it with something
Slovakian.

He looks at your wife, her soft smile still there, his eyes trying desperately to locate safety, assistance, an explanation.

He looks at you. You smile back at him, doing that hunchy
shoulder thing and raised eyebrow thing all at the same time,
which no doubt means the same in Slovakian as in English.

Sara pushes the handle of the fork again and Filip gives out
a yelp.

The two boys follow each other to the kitchen door and
stand there. Intent. They look at Sara, not taking their eyes
from her. Not even to look at Filip.

Sara doesn't say a word. The hint of a smile. She raises her
foot to the fork, draws it back, then gives an almighty kick with
her heel. Like she is digging potatoes. Filip grabs at the table in
pain, a low whine from his belly. He tries to stand, but the fork
is making it impossible for him to move beyond a crouch as it
lifts the chair when he straightens. Sara gives another kick and
he screams.

The boys laugh in unison and scatter back to the table
scrambling onto your knees to have a good view
and a cuddle.

He looks across at you again and shouts.

'Stop her. Please. Stop her.'

And you are amazed that he can still think to speak English

at such a time. Admirable really. You look straight at him and laugh.

What can you do but laugh?

Because it's funny! As if you would!

You look into Sara's face. The smile.   **Your wee girl.**

Filip's breath is becoming broken.

Your wife stands and walks round to the other side of the table, staring into Filip's face the whole time. He watches her till she is half way round, then Sara twists the fork out of his back. Filip folds onto the floor, shuffles back, hands and feet scratching into the corner. He leans his back against the large sideboard, against the warm wood. Closes his eyes.

Sara looks at the prongs of the fork, then up towards you. She looks straight through you – as if you are not there.

Your wife reaches Filip and he opens his eyes. Tries to stand but cannot manage. She bends down, lifts her hand to his cheek and strokes it. He cries, trying to hold her close, like a mother.

She looks up at Sara and nods.

Your wife steps away.

You and the boys stand up to get a better look.

Filip presses back against the sideboard. Breathing in bursts, he looks up at your wife, looks to Sara who is holding the fork aloft ... then thrusts it into his chest.

The look of disbelief on his face.

Sara looks across at you. Into your eyes. She leans on the fork as if it were a gatepost and smiles a wide smile.

Stephanie Green

THE LUNATIC LAUNDRESS
(Hanwell Asylum, 1834)

We each have our tasks:
the delirious wash
the aggressive wring it
the imbeciles hang up the linen to dry
the melancholy iron it
the obsessives fold it
and put it away.

I'm a washer and wringer
for they say I am violent,
curse, swear
and use bad language.
I'm kept busy from six in the morning
till late. I'm too busy to argue
or even to think.

It's better than sewing
sitting still as a statue
except for the needle
pricking the cloth
in and out
like what the master
did to me.

It's better than thinking
about my baby.
I must be docile
and pious
and grateful
to the parish
for taking her in.

I'll slap and I'll slap
till I've loosened the dirt
of my sin and am pure
as a nun,
my mind purged of madness
as blank as clean sheets
and neatly folded up.

Jen Hadfield

THRIMILCE – ISBISTER

*'The Anglo-Saxons called (May) thrimilce, because
then cows can be milked three times a day.'*

Brewer's Dictionary of Phrase and Fable

Cheddared, the light sealed
in rind of dry road;
bloom and sheen of the ditches
I've been dreaming all this life;
the close-quilled irises
rooted dense and deep
as flight feathers.

Recognition rises
– cream in a tilted pitcher.

Paul de Havilland

WIDOW

When the widow was sixty years old visitors started to come to her beach. Some came on foot, some in battered, rusting vehicles that seemed new and shining to her. She knew the visitors must be rich to travel so far (once or twice she and her husband had taken the ferry to Athens) and couldn't understand why they would sleep naked on the beach, listening to strange music by the campfire. Often they would sing to their own guitars and she liked to hear that, but sometimes loud crazy music would shake from the beaten-up vehicles. Then she would go to the beach and mime for them to quieten down, putting her hands over her ears then together in prayer. Usually they would smile and comply, but once they ran laughing up to her, and led her to their fire where she hid her eyes from the naked boys. They tried to make her dance and smoke. They laughed when she ran away, her head shaking and her hands in the air.

But this only happened once. Most of the time she liked to have them around. It broke the monotony which can take root in even the most beautiful surroundings after more than fifty years. Once or twice people wanted a room. They would mime their requests, and she would indicate her price by showing them crumpled notes from her purse, or scribbling it down. They would always laugh and shrug at each other incredulously, even after she had tripled her original price. (She couldn't in all conscience charge more.) She would wait until they were asleep before bedding herself down on the porch; always be up and about before them so they had no idea they had taken her bed; so she could keep their money and her pride.

Then the woman in black came, not a Greek widow's black but black all the same. A short black blouse, a gap, then a long black tight-fitting skirt buttoned down the front.

The widow was in her large arid garden, bent stiff-legged ninety degrees at the waist, picking peppers from her bushes. Absently she must have heard the approach and halt of footsteps, because she placed her hands on the back of her hips and pushed herself upright. She saw an attractive woman, a shy smile under a mop of boyishly cut red hair. A red that would look natural only on a fox.

The old lady was taken aback when the newcomer greeted

her in Greek and asked her where she might find a room. The
reply came in a torrent that would translate roughly as, 'Well
bless me. You speak Greek. How lovely. Well, it so happens I
might have a room, would you like to come in and we'll discuss
it?'

The young woman blinked at her, embarrassed. It was
obvious her Greek wasn't up to the reply and so the old lady
beckoned her into the house. Her prospective guest smiled, and
slid gracefully through the gate, under the fig tree to the porch.
Here her smile grew, and she reached up to stroke the leaves
and ripening fruit of the sheltering grape vine.

Inside were just two rooms, one with a fire for cooking, a
sink with a single tap, and a lace-covered table. The chairs were
in the other room along with a narrow bed and a great many
shelves of trinkets, and photographs and pictures all of people,
all looking sternly at the viewer. Lace filled every available
space like spray-painted cobwebs. The rooms were dark and
cool and fastidiously tidy. The girl hugged herself and smiled
broadly, 'How much?'; again in Greek. This time she appeared
to understand the old lady's reply. She sat in one of the chairs,
and fished in her backpack for a wallet. She counted out a sum
of money and presented it to her host. It was ten times what she
had asked, an enormous sum. Shaking her head, the old lady
again gave her price, stressing the hundreds which she assumed
the girl had heard as thousands and offering the money back.
The girl held up her hands, her fingers and thumbs fisted.
Chanting the price each time, she raised her fingers and thumbs
one by one. The old lady stared. Did she mean to stay for ten
days? This must be what she meant.

She considered. What would she do with a stranger in her
house for ten days? But how could she refuse the money? She
could buy her winter's fuel with it. But could she sleep on the
porch for ten days? The weather would be no problem at this
time of year. But what about mosquitoes? She would think of
something. She smiled, and put the money into a stone jar by
the door. The girl hugged herself again and spun round once in
joy. She held out her hand. 'Sandra,' she said. The old lady was
in something of a spin herself. Unused to the informality of first
names, she hesitated. But then she grinned, held out her hand
and said, 'Katerina.'

Katerina went back to her gardening, leaving her guest to
unpack. The first couple of days went without a hitch, the old

lady making sure Sandra was asleep before she bedded down, getting up early so she was always tending her plants when her guest rose.

On the third night, however, the game was up. Katerina was woken by Sandra's hand on her shoulder. Sandra looked her in the eye, frowning as she drew on her limited Greek. 'This,' she pointed at the door, 'your room.'

Katerina sat up and sighed. She tried to shoo Sandra back inside, but her guest would have none of it. She took Katerina by the hand and led her into her house. There was now a bed made up on the floor of an inflated li-lo and a sleeping bag, and Sandra gestured Katerina to her own bed. In reply Katerina went to the stone jar, counted out half the money and handed it to Sandra. Sandra looked at the refund, halved it again and gave Katerina back the rest. This negotiation satisfied Katerina and her pride, so after smiling and shaking hands again, they both spent the night indoors.

The next couple of days went by in an instantaneously adopted routine. Sandra dressed and left early in the morning, returned in the early evening looking windswept and sandy, then washed at the sink. Katerina spent the day tending her garden. The third evening she prepared a simple meal for both of them, having seen Sandra eat only bread, feta and tomatoes she must have bought in the village above the bay. Sandra ate with gusto and evident delight. Afterwards she washed up, then they sat in peaceful silence; Sandra smoking and Katerina making lace.

The next night Sandra was back very late. Katerina had spent the evening telling herself she was being stupid to worry; Sandra was not her daughter. Sandra went straight to bed. Katerina waited a while before doing so herself, to hide her concern.

A little later the peace of the night was broken by the sound of quiet sobbing. Katerina got out of bed, and lit the oil lamp. She sat on the floor next to Sandra, and said, 'Tell, speak.'

Sandra sat up, bleary from tears and halfway to sleep. She smiled, shook her head and reached up and squeezed Katerina's shoulder. Then she made to settle back down.

Katerina shook her gently to regain her attention. 'Tell, speak.'

Sitting up again, Sandra paused, as if thinking what to say or how to say it in Greek. Then she took Katerina's hand and pointed to the wedding ring. She gestured to the photos and pictures on the wall. 'Which?'

Katerina stood up, and took down a black and white photo of a handsome Greek boy in his mid-twenties, assuming the same stern expression as all the other faces captured around the walls. Sandra took the photo and smiled at it. 'He is gone now?' she said.

'Gone.' Katerina raised seven fingers, one for each year since his death.

Sandra pointed to herself. 'Mine too.' She held up a fist with no fingers raised. Then she grabbed Katerina in a bear hug, and sobbed for what seemed an age.

Sandra slept fairly late that morning. Katerina gathered some flowers from her garden, and packaged them up with candles and some matches. She prepared yoghurt and honey for breakfast, and made coffee when Sandra awoke. After breakfast she said to Sandra, 'Please, come with me today?'

'Where?'

'To my husband's shrine.'

This was too much for Sandra's Greek, so another game of charades followed. Katerina showed Sandra the candles and flowers, and pointed to her husband's photo, then she mimed walking. She held her arms wide to imply it was a long way. Sandra looked serious, then nodded.

The walk was long and hard, but very beautiful. Katerina led them along the coast for a way, then as the bay swept to their right she kept going, into the hills through pine, olive and cypress groves. Above, the mountains loomed, craggy rock cliffs scarring the tree-clad slopes.

After about an hour they turned onto a road clinging to the side of the hill. They followed the road, finally stopping at a sharp bend with a sheer drop beyond. There was the shrine, set into the rock face on the inside of the bend.

Sandra sat quietly as Katerina removed dead flowers, put fresh ones inside and lit the candles she had brought. When she had finished she went over to the edge of the road, and pointed down the cliff edge, her other arm sweeping to indicate an imaginary vehicle careering down the hill, and failing to make the bend.

'Yours?' she pointed at Sandra.

Sandra put her hand over her chest, and panted to indicate shortness of breath. Suddenly, she grinned at their pantomime. Katerina laughed, and walked toward Sandra wagging her head from side to side. When she reached her, though, they became serious and clasped each other's hands.

Katerina broke from Sandra's grip and reached down into her package. She gave Sandra a candle and indicated the shrine. Sandra nodded and went to the shrine and lit her candle. She watched it burning for a long while, then she went over to Katerina, took her by the hand and led her back down the road.

As they set off Katerina said, 'Yours, in England?'

Sandra stopped, looked at her and shook her head. She shrugged her shoulders. 'Yes,' she said. Then quietly, in English, 'So far as I know,' as they resumed their walk.

For the rest of her stay, Sandra and Katerina spent the days apart, but fell into the habit of having a companionable meal in the evenings. On the last evening, Sandra washed up after their meal, and then sat with Katerina.

Katerina knew this was their last night. She had mixed feelings. She would miss Sandra's company, but was looking forward to having her house to herself. Sandra produced an envelope, which she gave to Katerina. Katerina made to open it, but Sandra stopped her.

'Tomorrow, when I go,' she said.

Katerina smiled, and left the package sealed. Sandra was looking at her earnestly. 'I don't write. After I go, I don't write. I will think of you a lot.'

Katerina looked at this strange girl. She hadn't really imagined she would write to her. She felt fond of her, felt sorry for her loss, but Sandra puzzled her. Why would a young widow be travelling around the globe? Why was she on her own? Where were her family? Katerina had people all round her. Any time she wanted company, she could go up to the village and sit with her friends; she had cousins in the village. Her son in Athens was there if she needed him. She smiled at Sandra, 'I will think of you too.' And she would, she would pray for her.

The next morning when Katerina awoke, Sandra was already gone. She had heard her getting ready very early, but understood what she was doing and so had not stirred.

After her breakfast, she took Sandra's envelope and opened it. Inside was a candle, and a small photograph. At first it looked like Sandra herself, but when Katerina looked closer she could see it was a girl of the same age, but prettier, with dark eyes and a full mouth.

This then must be who died. Katerina was puzzled. Sandra had made it clear that the dead person was a husband, perhaps a fiancé. Even so, that evening she lit the candle by the photograph to honour Sandra's unspoken request.

The following morning Katerina looked up from her gardening to see a young couple peering shyly from the fence. She smiled. They greeted her with waves and nods, and the boy spoke the single Greek word, 'Room?'

Katerina, now a rich woman who could afford her solitude, shook her head. The visitors waved goodbye and walked off along the bay. Katerina watched them until they had disappeared, then wiped her hands on a rag by the door and went inside. She picked up the photo Sandra had left, and lifted the framed picture of her husband from the shelf. She smiled at them both, then tucked the girl between the glass and the corner of the frame before putting it back.

Linda Henderson

MOON FAT HERON

In Angus, which lies to the south and east of here, it is said that the size of a heron waxes and wanes with the moon. Plump moon; plump heron. But at the full moon, should you venture out to catch Heron, he will see you coming with your pole and your snare; if you use a flashlight he will take fright and waken the whole colony in raucous croaks of disdain. So, a full moon blinded by cloud is heron-catching time. Life is full of such frustrations.

For three full moons in succession Molly Lockhart had sent her lumbering son, Gillon, to catch a fat heron to provide them with a meal of meat and a crock of fat for the winter. For three full moons Gillon had followed his mother's instructions but returned each time empty-handed. He had practised the snaring technique on their own cockerel. The cock still crowed. He had practised on the cat asleep on the shed roof. The cat still slept, a little higher up the roof. He had practised on the dog. The dog had died, a grisly, garrotted death.

Molly cooked up the dog, for after all, meat is meat and she wanted her son to grow strong in the arm, if not in the head. He would hardly do that on sliced white bread and strawberry jam. But she kept the heart of the dog, wrapped it well in caul and put it on the high shelf in the larder to wait the next full moon.

Gillon went about the farm herding his uncle's sheep without the help of the dog. He found that if he approached quietly, crouching down, arms spread, as the ewes looked up uncertain if they should flee, he could take off towards them with a whooping noise and gather perhaps ten whose nature it was to huddle together rather than scatter, being so frightened by the spectacle to want to get into whatever shelter was on offer, and fast. By altering his speed and the amount and pitch of his whooping Gillon manoeuvred such a group into the fank and clicked the gate closed. Breathing hard he took a clean white linen handkerchief from his pocket and wiped his brow. Gillon cared not for personal hygiene and didn't notice the rank animal stench of his clothes but every day he carried a clean white linen handkerchief. He had bought three dozen from a catalogue run by Mrs MacInnes at the Post Office, paying a pound a week for twenty weeks. At each new moon (it being much less busy than at the full) he would fill a bucket with boiling water, add a scoop of washing powder from a box that he had bought specially; powder that the box claimed would soak out any biological stain man could produce, and stir in his dirty hand-kerchiefs with a half length of broom handle. They swirled and swirled and the water took on the colour and consistency of the cream of mushroom soup that his mother bought dried in packets from the shop.

The shop stocked packet soups, a few tins of vegetables, plain biscuits, sliced white bread and strawberry jam. Molly Lockhart went daily for soup, tinned marrowfat peas and sliced white bread. There were three varieties of soup; cream of mush-room, tomato and spring vegetable, which Gillon didn't like so they alternated tomato and cream of mushroom. Molly watched her budget; there was no point in spending more than was needed for that day. What if she died in the night and had wasted money stocking up on packets of soup that Gillon had no idea how to make? Best to leave them on the shop shelf until they were needed. She collected butter and milk from the farm dairy as part of Gillon's wages and the hens gave them a few eggs each day in summer.

When Gillon's handkerchief soup was thick and starting to grow a surface skin he would fill another bucket with cold water and, using the stick, carefully transfer each item from the wash to the rinse. Then it was stir, stir, stir again. Fully focussed on the restored whiteness of his shoal of handkerchiefs he would repeat the rinsing in a third bucket and then feel able to sink his hands into the water as though guddling for trout, and lift each one out, give it a gentle squeeze, pull it square and peg it on the line he'd rigged twice round the kitchen. There, twen-ty-eight flags would drip overnight and he would rise early the next morning to iron and fold them as his mother had shown him. He stored them in a box in his room that came with a pair of slippers Molly had from the catalogue. Out of the original three dozen there were still four untouched, waiting to replace any that Gillon thought no longer came up to standard. Oil marks and blood seemed hard to remove.

Happy to have ten sheep collected, Gillon looked up to see yet fifty dotted about the field, settled and grazing now, but ready to jump and dance and weave to escape Gillon's out-spread arms. By the end of the day there were nineteen in the fank but with no ready water supply and rain coming on, which would leave the fleeces too wet for shearing, the farm manager told Gillon to release the sheep back into the field. Life is full of such frustrations.

'So, Gillon,' said his mother, 'it's raining and it's a full moon tonight. Heron will be squat down in his nest and you will have no light. But you must go for I am hungry for some tasty flesh and for some fat to rub on my arthritic joints. I have chopped a little of the dog's heart into this cloth.' Gillon recognised one of his discarded handkerchiefs.

'Move quietly up under the nest and lay a little heart on the rim. Heron will smell it and stretch his neck to take it. Then lay a little more. Get his confidence. And when Heron stretches his long shaggy neck over your head you tempt him a little more with a morsel on the snare wire. And, just as he snatches at it, you strike!'

Gillon looked at the heart and was about to tell her it wouldn't work because herons have no sense of smell and don't feed at night but he decided it would make for a quieter life if he just went along with it. Perhaps he would net a salmon instead. He set off in the direction of the heronry but turned at the bottom of the hill and went towards the river. But even from the track he could see the ghillie's flashlight letting poachers know that he was about. The rain had passed but the moon was still obscured by cloud. Gillon knew every inch of the slopes and found by instinct, rather than by vision, a rocky shelter hidden by tall heather just above the riverbank. He tucked himself into it and slept through the short hours of darkness.

When he woke it was to a fresh blustery day with the sun already pushing above the plantation that covered all the hills to the east. Heron was at the water's edge on the opposite bank. Now, if he could tempt the bird to cross over by wiggling the heart on the end of the pole he could yet waken his mother with the tickle of a grey feather.

He pulled the cloth, now brown and sticky, from his left pocket (his clean white linen handkerchief was always in his right) and collected some straggly moss from the damp crease of ground at the bottom of the slope. Lying on his belly, hoping that Heron wouldn't spot him, he twined a length of the slippery heart with the fibrous moss root and secured it around the snare wire. He laid the pole out at full stretch and shuffled down the bank on his stomach into a position where he could extend the pole out over the river above a bank of shingle. By gently twitching the pole he could make the heart wriggle and seem to be alive. It didn't look much like a frog or an eel to him but he wasn't a heron. Heron's eyes swivelled and spotted breakfast. It was an eel; a small eel, yes, but wriggling and grounded on the shingle; easy pickings. He lifted a large claw cautiously out in front of him, waited, sank it into the water and lifted the other. Gillon held his breath. Heron stalked across the shallows and with one lightning movement stabbed the heart and gobbled it down. Excited, Gillon withdrew the pole ever so slowly and re-baited. This time he chose a spot on a muddy tussock that had fallen from the bank where the river had undercut it. What Heron saw was a frog jump from the water. He stalked and fed again. Heron was now barely an arm's length away.

Gillon thought that the best way to snare Heron would be to lay the circle of wire on the very edge of the bank with the last of the meat in the middle. Holding the pole in his right hand would leave his stronger left hand free to yank the wire closed at just the right moment, matching his reaction speed to Heron's. The knack was in pulling the wire at an angle out from the pole so that it ran freely through the little steel gate then, with it tight around its victim, dropping the hand back to the pole to lock the gate. This was more secure than the simple running noose method they'd used before when any slackness of grip might allow a bird to work the knot loose and escape. Wire had long since replaced plaited horse-hair. His mother had designed the locking mechanism after seeing how the venetian blinds in the Big House kitchen worked. She'd told Gillon to find some ball-bearings in the tractor shed. Then she'd filed grooves in them and set one in the end of the pole with an opposing stop. Pulling the wire away from the pole opened the gap and let it run in a groove in the ball. On bringing the wire parallel to the pole the gap was closed, clenching the wire tight. This freed both of the catcher's hands. Molly had sat at the kitchen table, night after night, practising on a leek tied to the back of a chair until she was satisfied the design was merciless.

Gillon visualised the wire cutting Heron's slender neck and the fat body keeling over. How pleased his mother would be, perhaps let him rest his head in her lap as he'd done as a boy. She would stroke his hair and tell him he would grow fine and strong.

He opened the cloth in his palm and plumped up the heart to make it look like a ball of worms. All the time he barely breathed as Heron still stared at the tussock waiting for another frog. Gillon pushed the snare pole slowly to the bank's edge, and then extended his other arm, palm uppermost, with the cloth and its treasure ready to be slipped into the ring's open mouth. Heron's eyes swivelled even though his head didn't move. There was a ball of worms coming into view to his right side. Really, this morning was proving to be an easy feast. With a sideways lunge, stretch and strike he pierced the offering, the handkerchief and Gillon's hand. Gillon leapt up, screamed and danced with the pain. Heron took off, crying 'frarnk, frarnk' with the cloth still dangling from his beak. Gillon sat on the bank and nursed his hand. When the pain passed into numbness he decided that it would be worth the sacrifice of his clean hand-kerchief to bind the wound. He hugged his hand inside his jacket and walked home to a breakfast of sliced white bread and strawberry jam and cold comfort from his mother.

Still Molly was determined that a moon fat heron would be hers before winter. She divided the rest of the dog's heart into three and went to the riverbank each morning to tempt Heron. She could move as quietly and wispily as a fairy messenger, sidling up to Heron and dangling slivers of the meat from her fingers. Then she would withdraw as silently as she'd come leaving Heron to fish in peace. Gillon wanted no further part in this and vowed that he wouldn't let the meat pass his lips even if Heron could be caught.

When all of the dog's heart had gone Molly went begging to the kitchen of the Big House. The Big House, the farm, the estate and Molly's cottage were owned by her brother, but he visited only two or three times a year with his pretty Brazilian wife and his 'butter wouldn't melt' children. At the kitchen door Lizzie the Cook said she would look out for some offal for Molly and to call in on Saturday afternoon. Molly thought that there must be a sheep or deer being killed for the larder and said she hoped for a little heart but that liver or even intestines would do. Lizzie said she couldn't promise but would see what was left. When Lizzie got to the supermarket in Dundee on Saturday morning there was no fresh offal on display. With all the regulations and mad cows people didn't want to eat guts much, although Lizzie herself was ever partial to liver and onions. All she could find were tubs of frozen chicken livers she sometimes bought to make paté. These would have to do. Molly should know they could no longer kill their own meat. Life is full of such frustrations.

Lizzie was rather late back and, realising she'd probably missed Molly, put the tubs in the big chest freezer. She'd make a batch of paté if Molly didn't want them.

Molly had estimated that if she went to the kitchen at about four o'clock Lizzie might invite her in for tea and a blether, but when there was no reply she reverted to her view that Lizzie bowed and scraped a little too much to Molly's brother. She had just been putting Molly off because she didn't want to be bothered with her or was afraid of the laird's temper. Molly stalked home empty-handed and angry. She took out the snub on Gillon, making him clean out the hen house, a foul job that they both hated.

That evening, as the sun was setting and Gillon went to light the smoky oil lamps (his uncle provided no electricity to the cottage), there was a sharp tapping at the cottage door. They never had visitors; no one from the Big House ever came to them and there was no road nearby for hawkers or lost tourists to trouble them. The tap came again; louder, low down. Molly bade Gillon answer the door, for she was a little afraid. He tried to see who was there by pressing his cheek to the window but it was already too dark. He lifted the latch and scraped back the door just as Heron was pulling his head back to tap for the third time.

'Oh! Come in, Master Heron.' cried Molly, thinking this was too good to be true and starting to plan her trap and smell roasting heron. Heron stepped into the room and up to the kitchen table while Gillon stood holding the door ajar.

'Master Heron. I am so sorry I've not been able to bring you heart these last two days. Gillon will run up to the Big House and see if Lizzie the Cook has something for you.' Molly threw a burning glance at Gillon while smiling at Heron.

Gillon arrived at the kitchen door to find it open, the lights on but no one around. There was no food laid out so he went to the larder hoping a rabbit or pheasant would be hung there, but the larder was bare. He had watched Lizzie putting dishes into the chest freezer when he'd been up at the house collecting his wages. He lifted the lid and saw the pots of chicken livers. He didn't know that's what they were as he couldn't read the label, and they didn't look like the liver he'd seen his mother pull from the inside of a hen when it ended its laying life and went into a stew. But they had the colour of meat of some kind. There were three pots. Sure that one wouldn't be missed he juggled it in his still-sore hand, finally tucking it under his arm. He lowered the freezer lid and slipped back out into the night.

Gillon trudged home hoping that by the time he arrived Heron might have escaped and that whatever it was in the pot under his arm his mother could make into a supper for them. But when he opened the door, there was Molly on one side of the table and Heron on the other, their eyes fixed on him. He put the pot on the table and retreated into the shadows to watch.

'Come, Master Heron,' said Molly. 'Do help yourself.' She pushed the pot towards him, removed the lid and held it up to the oil lamp. The label said 'Best Chicken Livers' and under the heading 'Ingredients' it added 'chicken livers'. She was glad she had not read this aloud as she wasn't sure whether Heron would be happy eating the vitals of a fellow bird but, at the same time, she hoped he would not take all of them, for chicken livers fried in a little butter and served on toast are quite delicious. Heron swivelled his eyes to focus on the unpromising pot. There was no sign of movement, no sense that there had been life in the pot at all recently; but surely that was blood running around the edge? He lifted his head a little and took a gentle, polite stab. Gillon winced as a pain shot through his hand. Heron's steel-sharp bill made no impression on the frozen surface and in that moment, the moment when an animal is at its most vulnerable; in that moment when Heron instinctively swivelled his eyes backwards to check; in that moment he spotted the snare wire falling towards his head. The bird put up an awful croaking, opened his wings and flapped hard sending Molly falling backwards with the snare pole flailing out behind her. As she tried to regain her feet and bring it back over her head she pulled the wire hard against the pole, and felt the noose catch round something. She pulled again and Gillon fell forward between herself and Heron, blood seeping through the incised wound forming a red smile at his neck.

Heron flapped hard enough to take off, flew straight at the window, breaking it out of its frame and escaped towards the moon. Molly would have to wait yet another month. Life is full of such frustrations.

Brent Hodgson

AN ECCLESIASTICAL SONG IN PRAISE OF KARROTTES

Karrottes, high in sugar energy and karotene,
Karrottes, European biennial of white flower.
Karrottes, you give me pleasure each and every day.
Karrottes, you are a true friend to all Mankind.
Karrottes, you are better for the health than a jar of heather honey.
Heather honey is sweet but Karrottes are better for the health.
Blueberry jam is blue but Karrottes are red which suits me fine.
Karrottes, you grow deep down in the earth.
Karrottes, I love you.

If like me you love a Karrotte,
You will love a Karrotte with all your heart and soul.
If like me you love a Karrotte
You will keep a Karrotte in your bedroom;
A Karrotte will restore your sight should you go blind.
If like me you love a Karrotte
You will keep a Karrotte in your pocket;
A Karrotte will get you walking should you go lame.
If like me you love a Karrotte,
You will take a Karrotte with you on your summer holiday.
And if like me you love a Karrotte,
You would lose your right leg to save the Karrottes of the world,
And I would fight many a battle with those evil bastards
Who give Karrottes a bad name.

Karrottes of the world!
Send your roots deep down in the earth,
Send your green petals into the sky.
Karrottes of the world!
May you never become untasty,
May you never become untrustable.
Karrottes of the world!
You are the bringer of vitality,
You are the bringer of first-class eyesight.
Karrottes of the world!
When I feel a vitamin deficiency coming on
I run into the garden and it is you I pluck.
Karrottes of the world, I love you.

The *Daucus karota* is the Karrotte
Mighty member of the Ombrella family,
With a high sugar content and full of karotene;
Eaten in Europe since the sixteenth century.

Sad are they who do not have a Karrotte on which to chew.
Sad are they who do not love the Karrotte
With all their heart and soul.
Listen to these words carefully, boys and girls;
Don't you ever kick a Karrotte in the teeth,
The wind will blow away your Tom Cruise posters if you do,
The waves of the blue-green-grey ocean will flood your bedroom
Then on your little heads the sky shall fall.

Karrottes, with your red root straight and tapering,
You are a true friend of all Mankind.
You are better to eat than a slimy fish,
You are without a single bone,
And who wants to eat smelly fish anyway.

Once I was a human wreck without a Rolls-Royce to my name,
Then Karrottes came into my life, now I am a billionaire!
I do not wish to bullshit you but Karrottes are dear to me;
They mean more to me than wearing Boots No 7 lipstick.

Karrottes, every day I sing in praise of you.
Here is a simple truth of which I sing;
You have a high sugar content.
Here is a second truth of which I sing;
My liver looks for you to convert your karotene into vitamin A.
Karrottes, I thank the day you came into my life
And made me almost as rich as Bill Gates.
Karrottes, mighty member of the Ombrella family,
You are red root vegetable.
You grow deep down in the earth
Where you become plump and esculent.
Karrottes, with your pretty petals and gorgeous root
You are more fun than a game of dominoes.
Karrottes, I love you.

Carla Jetko

KITCHEN AUBADE

When I woke up under the great plank table
I knew I would have to say goodbye;
kiss your purple painted eyelids
to the smell of bacon frying.

One cook was already scraping a cast-iron pan
across a burner. His crepe-soled shoes
stepped on the spread of your black hair
but didn't wake you.
Your chest created gentle waves
under the garland of plastic gardenias you wore
from the night before.
I stole an apron off the Aga handle, and covered you.
I waited until everyone had left the room
and then crept out
with a croissant crumbling warm in my mouth.

Allan Knox

SHELL SUITS

Scotland's National Dress
Cheap
Reliable
Available
Oaps!
Loass ma pen
Foon annar yin
Aye –
Available fi any pub
Cheap cos it wis choarried
Nae wunner
Minimum wage
What dae they expect?
Perks ae the joab
PAUKKULL
No jiss the shell suit mind
ACCESSORIES
Moby
Wee hat
Turned up the wuy
Barry Ferguson style
Rangers shell suit
Oan Bothwell Bridge
Eftir the derby
'*Ya fud*'
Like oan 'Off the Ball'
Wi thoan Tam Cowan
In Cosgrove
Big man in the media
Ex-casual
Best hing aboot the shell suit though
Easy tae light!

Norman Kreitman

DAFT GEORGIE

He came off that bike two years ago, since when
anyone will tell you he's daft.
Why else drag one leg, clench tight
against the ribs a claw instead of a hand?
Ask him a question, and he'll only grunt.

Yet somehow he fetches himself along the close,
scraping that lazy foot.
Anyone can hear him shuffle-shuffle near,
and the boys hoot from the doorways,
tilt their heads and crooning like apes

form a column to jiggle in line behind him.
And not-so daft Georgie marvels
at the impatience of these mimics,
each rehearsing the hemiplegia
which time is keeping in store for anyone.

MR PINK'S AFTERNOON

O life, O forest, O sunlight, O youth, O hopes.
— Alexei Tolstoy

The moods of my neighbour, Mr Pink,
are usually subjunctive. He draws me aside,
whispers 'Oh, would that it were otherwise.' That
is what he says.

Since he retired from the bank
blocks of neutral time confront him
from which to build fine monuments, complete
with battlements and spires:

meanwhile it's Tuesday afternoon
and stays that way. Frequently he plans
to drive to Kenya, there to encounter lions. Instead
he glares at the wall

putting the evil eye
on luckless spiders. But sometimes, more cheerful,
he calls out 'What's wrong with here that isn't wrong
with everywhere?'

The question gives him satisfaction.
And just today he called 'Aha'. That, smiling,
is what he said. 'I got up and mowed the lawn.
Tiring, but I'll enjoy

my nap the more.' *O life, O forest, O sunlight, etc. etc.*

Helen Lamb

LATE NOW

she breathes him out
she breathes him in
spirit seeps between her thighs
his ear is so near
and so far away
too late now to whisper
why she came here

she breathes him in

REVOLVING DOOR

he pulls her in
and round they go

between the comfort of the foyer
and the restless ringing alley

and he shoves
round-round they go

between the laughter back in the bar
the dangerous need in a whisper

between the opening they're looking for
the swift relief of departure

and he shoves
she brakes

they stumble together
onto the definite pavement

Douglas Lipton

ALLAN

I am in the darkness
breathing and staring
into it before sleep.
Under the bed
I can hear Allan
shuffling his claws
flicking his tail
like castanets
as he unsettles.
Allan is the size of me
and lives there all the time.
Unlike most of his kind
he doesn't need water
to lurk in. He just lies there
smiling whatever his mood
(although he has no moods
apart from hunger).
Here and there a fang
hangs through to impale something.

When I sleep like a door
the rats begin to enter.
They dart about the carpet
until they walk into the yawning
gulf of Allan's odourless mouth.
Clench. Gulp. Clench. Gulp.
That's how it goes on all night.
It's so simple for him.
The rats don't realise he's there,
for at night he's so cold
and colourless and silent,
like a piece of furniture.
He makes no appeal
to their senses,
so the simpering rats
are entrapped.

It is easy for me
to take care of Allan,
ready and steady as a jamb.
Every night while I sleep,
he's there. In the morning
I say hello to him, and give him
a big bowl of water
before I head for school.
I don't know what he does all day,
except come out
from under the bed
to bathe in the sunlight
and grow.

Christine De Luca

EXISTENTIAL PARAGLIDIN IN TURKEY

Tinkin on da haert's topography
– heichts wir climmed, jimpit aff a,
aa but miracklin wirsels,
brinks o banks wir teetered apön –
wir blyde da day we hae na da pooster
fur paraglidin. Da aeriel photos
takk wir braeth awa, shaa
da hale pictir. Aert-fast, wir laerned
da bird's-eye view da herd wye,
bit bi bit, graftin a life tagidder,
backwirds, makkin hit fit.

O FOR DA WINGS
Tae da unnamed builder o Woodwick doocot, Orkney

Dy doocot staands, a chapel noo;
nae currie-coo, nae flaachter
o gluffit wings, nor guff o doos.

Smooth, dark flags; flör ta röf boxed
wi steyn skelfs lik doorless presses.
An ivery steyn set sae is ivery skelf
is tae da waa an tae da biggin
is ivery filament is tae da fedder
an tae da doo; ivery bit a wirk o art.

Did du bigg hit, i da mind, a library
fur books o air, wi winged servitors
ta rekk ta tapmost skelfs; ta hoose
da silence o a thoosand vellum scrolls,
sneck raised only bi a holy haand?

Whin at last du laid da hidmist steyn
du man a steppit back, apö da seevent day
an, luikin wi da speirin een o wan at kens
da human haert, du man a kent at whit
du'd med, dis testament, wis göd.

Lynda McDonald

AN ALLOTMENT IN EDEN*

Noah sent out the raven first,
which flew about in agitation.
So instead he sent the dove three times.
The first time it could not settle.
The second it brought an olive branch.
The third time it never returned.

The railway came in 1884.
Sliced through green pastured Eden.
Through the lands of Canaan.
Onto Little Egypt.
Down the valley of the Nile.
Parting seas of cows, who reacted with tremulous panic,
nodding to each other from opposite banks
of the railway bed. Believing that each meadow
of buttercup, clover, sweet cicely, looked more tempting
on the other side.

After the heat had died down, came in turn,
the willow-herb, nettle, ragwort, bramble,
mansions, flats, shops, cars.
An absence of mystified cows.
And from the beak of one grey dove,
a tiny seed of crab-apple, bitter, self-contained.

For the people on the train had glimpsed
that it was good, this fruitful countryside.
And buildings went on and multiplied, until
only a triangle of land was left,
hugging the embankment,
in the long late shadows
of retirement flats.
So in the ancient of days, could be glimpsed
the last remaining piece of the puzzle,
of where the countryside went.

Two by two of everything radiated from the gravelled brink.
Neat, productive, tended by an unseen hand.
A pigeon loft for birds, which, unmoved by the habit of trains,
Prinked and preened in all their rural bliss,
waiting to bring back other instances of green.

Derelict now. The towering stems of cabbages
gone to seed, nod.
The passengers without distraction, nod.
One last bead-eyed pigeon watches from the crab-apple tree.

*Eden, Canaan, Nile and Little Egypt form an area in south Edinburgh

Stuart Robert Macdonald

CLICK

There were four exposures left in his camera
so I finished off the film.

A winter coast scene, ice-edged pools. Click.
Hovering grey gulls working the keen northerly. Click
A watery sun polishing the cropped law. Click
A flat rock stitched with white lichen, limpets. Click.

He had taken the children to the Mull of Galloway,
they were on holiday from the school.

The stunted lighthouse at the fingertip of grass and cliff.

The silent red foghorn.

Isle of Man, north coast of Ireland on a cold blue day.

Throatsome geese beside a single-track road,
the emerald grass waving like the Irish Sea.

Half-eaten apples, a melting bar of chocolate.

A kestrel hanging over a rotting fence post.

Portpatrick. The camera-bold row of houses at the pier.

To be inside his uncluttered eye on those last days as
his toe-hold s l i p p e d
from the land he'd never left.

Ian McDonough

THRILLER

Upstairs, Mr Eaves is penning a thriller.
His storyline is waltzing,
Fur-hatted,
Through the snowbound streets,
Pausing only to examine cryptic clues.

He threads a solemn maid
Into the fabric of the plot.
Her skirt hitched high
She ministers
To the pressing needs of spies
While finishing her thesis
On kittens and their role in espionage.

He sketches in a double agent,
Whose probing fingers
Build a timing device
So subtle
That even Mr Eaves
Is helpless to defuse it.

To his surprise, the storyline decides
That Mr Eaves has run clean out of ink.
The dishes in his sink
Are piling high, his characters
Refuse to stand in darkened doors,
Are bored with espionage,
Form writers circles,
Deconstruct his text.

Mr Eaves begins to sweat profusely,
Feels a creeping
Dampness in his pants
And watches
As his cold war draws
Incontinently to an end.

James McGonigal

from THE LITTLE BOOK OF DAYS

The Little Poem's Awake
The little poem of Saturday is spun
In the washing machine and flicked out
With a snap of the wrist instead of ironing
To hang on the radiator until morning.

For hours it listens in the darkened house,
To reconstruct a rhythm out of sonorous
Intakes and snore tones, and whatever it was
One of us shouted out twice in a dream.

Sunday Best
The little poem of Sunday puts on its glasses
Which have been polished by the cloth of hope
That leaves a sheen like light on the pond
In the park where ducks clip through haloes

And round which we walk on Sunday mornings
Knowing each line of the water's text, and singing it.
And round which we stroll on Sunday evenings
Re-reading each line of the text and changing it.

Monday's Lines
The little poem of Monday is hung out by its tail,
Something like a shirt dripping something like tears.
What it enjoys is ice on the wind, birdsong
Beyond oxters, gold parsnips socketed in earth.

What it gets is the back green squeezing
Fingers of grass between rollers of clay.
The poem watches their tips stretching
Out of the depths for a touch of its tears.

Where Did Tuesday Go?
The little poem of Tuesday got lost
Somewhere between the microwave
And the washing machine or else the corner
Of my eye and the colour of yours.

Was it a green or a hazel or a deep
Grey shade? Why can I not give
A clearer description to the police constable
Who looks earnestly round for my poem?

Mary McIntosh

A TIDY DAITH

Whit metters,
this auld cat deein
in a winter sun-blink,
a cannle flichter
in her bleck bool een.

Nae kist nor kirk
tae mark her weygane,
but grey glaur
makkin a skrankie shrood

as corbies claik a coronach
frae the brainches o a bonnet fir.

KIRRIE DEN

Camsteery chaffies
chirple bairnsangs.
Trees soughin lang-kept
secrets
owerhing bruckle grund.
Time tricklin
intae the linn.

A squirrel
snuffs deid air,
syne jinks aneth
STRANGE WURLD
pented
on the bandstand waa.

Martin MacIntyre

AOGASG NA H-IGHINN UIBHISTICH

Nighean Uibhisteach, ort aogasg an aoibhneis
Ann an dìomhaireachd taigh bràthair d' athar:
tha na dualan seunta gam fuasgladh air anfhadh na pìoba,
Is their na coigrich gur ro-mhaiseach, 'g amharc do ghnùis.

Nighean Uibhisteach, ort aogasg a' mhaslaidh
measg òigridh an t-saoghail mhòir Bhadhlaich:
cha mhùchar an dorran sin tha a' lasradh do chuim
Is ag imlich cuailein nach ceil ort tuar do chràidh.

Nighean Uibhisteach, ort aogasg an iongnaidh
Ann an Sabhal Mòr na h-aiseirigh Gàidhlig:
sannt gun dùil air taitneas toradh do bheòil,
d'fhalt donn gleansach a' taisbeanadh fradharc do shùilean.

Nighean Uibhisteach, ort aogasg do thrèibh Cheiltich
Ann an Uibhist Eireannach saor bho mhì-ghean;
tha do ghruag an-diugh geàrrte ri modh Bhaile Atha Cliath
is cainnt Chonamara cur fairis o bhilean làn feòl'.

FACES OF A UIST GIRL

Uist girl, you wear a joyful face
in the secrecy of your uncle's house:
your timid locks are unleashed on the breath of the pipes:
strangers remark how stunning is a glimpse of your countenance.

Uist girl, you wear an embarrassed face
midst the youth of the large world of Benbecula:
the welling is not tamed which flames around your chest,
and licks at the fringe which can not hide the colour of your pain.

Uist girl, you wear a perplexed face
in The Big Barn of the Gaelic Resurrection:
unexpected envy for the pleasantness of your mouth's fruits,
your brown gleaming hair revealing your eyes' sight.

Uist girl, you wear the face of your Celtic race
in an Irish Uist freed from sadness;
your hair is now cut in the styles of Dublin,
with the language of Conamara overflowing from full-fleshed lips.

EAGLAIS GA SAORADH FHÈIN

Chualas feadh an taighe faram-bualaidh.
Taigh a sgeadaicheadh do Dhia air saidhbhreas lom.
Dia a thug na buinn leis, 's fhada on uair sin,
Nach d'fhuiling bhith an còir an duibh sin ann.

Thogadh feadh nam marbh gaoir nan salm
Mairbh bha ro dheònach seinn gu binn
Deòin nach d' rinn a mhùchadh beatha na h-ùrach,
Daonnan daingeann, dìleas a dh' aindeoin tìm.

Chan fhacas len cuid sùilean teampall falamh
Sùilean bha ri at o bhroinn an ceann
Is at nan ad 's nach toilleadh meud a' ghràis sin
A bheir air naomh a mhac a mhurt le lann.

Is shàth is shàth is shàth iad ann a' chèile
Uidheaman air iasad bhon an Deamhan
Is dhearbhadh nuair dhòirteadh fuil a' Chrìosdaidh
Gu robh iad ceart, is ceart, ro-cheart nam batal-bròin.

CHURCH FREEING HERSELF

There was heard throughout the house, the thunder of pounding.
A house adorned for God with starkest wealth.
A god who scarpered long ago
unable to endure such proximity to black.

The wail of the psalms was raised amidst the dead,
dead who were all too willing to sing sweetly,
a will which life under the earth had not quenched.
Always steadfast, stalwart, unmoved by time.

Their eyes did not perceive the empty temple
eyes that were bulging from the inside of their minds
and the bulge of the bonnets which could not contain such a
                                        quantity of grace,
as allows a saint to spear his son to death.

And then they thrust and thrust and thrust into each other,
tools and weapons borrowed from the Devil
and it was proved at the spill of Christian blood,
that they were right, right, too right in their desperate crusade.

David S. Mackenzie

MICHAEL

I have started to cheat at cards. It's difficult to tell whether
Michael realises this yet because he doesn't say very much. In
fact Michael says very little indeed. Even if he is aware that I've
started to cheat he might say nothing. Saying nothing is what he
is good at; he does it most of the time. Of late he's been saying
even less than usual and I have noticed, with this retreat
towards complete silence, a decline in his ability to play cards. I
should explain, then, that I have begun to cheat because I want
to lose. I want to help Michael to win.

Michael is sixty-three. He is very thin and stooped. His
head is bald on top, with a fringe of thick grey hair that sticks
out at odd angles because he rarely combs it. He shaves every
three or four days so when we meet he usually has a thick
white uneven stubble. When he does shave he often misses
bits which grow longer till the next time. His face is pinched,
his lips thin and drawn; his permanent expression is that of
someone deeply troubled.

He has a coat, a heavy dark blue overcoat with wide lapels
that flap in the wind. The coat is filthy; he wipes his nose on
the sleeve. From one pocket protrudes a small grey towel.
When more than a wipe is needed he blows his nose on this
towel and rubs his face with it. Sometimes he hangs it over the
radiator to dry.

Surprisingly, his hands are small and delicate although the
fingernails are heavy and none too clean. His fingers are
yellowed from nicotine. I watch his hands carefully as he deals
the cards. The pack is old and greasy and I find them difficult
to deal. Michael has no problem; his actions are quick and
smooth and even. Fifteen cards: seven to me, eight for himself.
Come on then, Michael, what have you dealt me this time?

He has dealt me the three and seven of hearts, the ace and
seven of diamonds and the two, ten and king of spades. This is
good because, although I have two sevens and, with the ten and
king of spades, perhaps the beginning of a run, the hand has little
to offer. As usual, we are playing first to ten wins and I'm already
leading six–two. *Michael*, I say, *what crap have you dealt me this
time?* I shake my head. He glances up from his cards very briefly
then studies them again. He discards the seven of clubs.

I decide to pick it up. I throw away the ace of diamonds. Michael leaves this and takes the top card from the pack. He looks at it for a short while and then throws it down. It's the queen of spades.

I pick up the queen, throw away the two. Michael thinks hard about the two, decides to pick it up.

Suddenly, after only two cards, I have a very good hand – three sevens and a possible run. I only need the jack of spades and I've won.

It's Michael's turn to discard. He throws down the jack of spades.

So here is my dilemma: do I pick up the card and win or do I let it go? And what will be the effect on my relationship with Michael either way? When it comes down to it, what do I want my relationship with Michael to be? Here is a man I play cards with for a couple of hours every Saturday. We say almost nothing to each other during that time. We play cards and I win. I always win. Does Michael hate me for this? I don't think so. He is always here ready to play. He expects me to be here. If I'm late, the first hand is already dealt and he's sitting waiting for me, the cards in two untidy piles before him, seven for me, eight for him. He is waiting for me and will not look at his own hand till I arrive because that is not done. I look, now, at this tired and troubled and silent man, rather dirty, dressed in Salvation Army handouts, who chooses to apply the rules of card-playing rigorously. Between us lie the main pack, neatly stacked face down, and, face up, the jack of spades.

And I make my decision.

But it's too late anyway. Michael is placing his cards down on the table carefully, face up: two and four of spades, three eights and two jokers. As jokers are wild, Michael has won.

You bastard, I tell him. *Look at that.* I show him my cards, placing his discarded jack of spades in the run. *Beaten by a whisker.*

He smiles. He gathers the cards together, hesitates for a moment and then pushes them towards me. Six–three, my deal.

Michael drags from his pocket the soiled towel and blows his nose. After he has put the towel away again, he reaches into his other pocket and draws out a packet of cigarettes. He flips the lid open and offers me one. I thank him and tell him I don't smoke. I've been meeting Michael once a week for nearly eighteen months now and he still cannot remember this.

But then this is my interpretation. Perhaps his offer of a cigarette has nothing to do with memory. He draws one out for himself and puts the pack away. He tears the filter tip off the end of the cigarette and tosses it into the large metal ashtray. He lights up and sucks hard on the raw edge of the tobacco a couple of times and then puts the cigarette down. But he doesn't rest it on the edge of the ashtray; he drops it in the middle where it lies flat on top of the ash and butts that are already there.

Now is the time for me to speak. I am dealing the cards. I can speak now because Michael is free to reply. If I try to talk to him while he is dealing, he loses track of how many cards have been dealt, how many still to go. He doesn't get angry at this, he just stops and fidgets through the cards to see what point he has reached. If I ask him questions during the course of the play, it puts him off his game and he doesn't know whose turn it is to discard or pick up. So, if I want to speak, it must be now, while I am dealing. The trouble is that I can make mistakes too. Then it's Michael's turn to correct me. This he does with gestures if at all possible. It's as if speech is to be a last resort. I'm cruel to him. I feign ignorance. *What's wrong?* I ask. *Card,* he says at last, tapping his hand of six. *Too many?* I say. *More,* he says. *One more.* I deal him another one, pick up my own hand. *And you,* he says, waving a finger at me. *Me? Another card? Two,* he says, *two,* and his eyes are worried and his troubled look is more troubled than ever as if this were potential tragedy and loss. *Two,* I say. *Right.* And I take two from the top of the pack. *Two. OK.* We study our cards and his expression of anguish relaxes somewhat as he sorts his hand.

But now it is six–three and my deal. *So how's your place?* I ask. *Fine,* he says. Two cards. *No problems? No.* Four cards. *Have you used your cooker yet? No.* Six. *Why not?* He shrugs. *Uh.* I pause. *You've got to eat, Michael. Why not cook? Can you cook? I cooked...* he begins. *I cooked...* He shakes his head. He is tired of the subject already. *What did you cook?* I insist. *Beans once,* he says. I deal four cards; that makes ten. *You need more than beans, Michael. Last year,* he says. I laugh at this. Twelve cards. *Is that one plate of beans a year, is that it?* There is the flicker of a smile. Fourteen cards. And one more for me. *That's it,* he says. The hand is dealt.

I win two hands in a row. Eight–three. But I say seven–three and Michael agrees. By duping him in this way, fiddling with the numbers, perhaps I'm just confusing him further, adding to his difficulties. Why is it so important to me to get him to win? But it's seven–three now, not eight–three. It's seven–three and I can't go back. Seven–three and first to ten is the winner. I collect the cards and pass them across the table. *A cup of tea, Michael?* I ask. I know what his response will be. He will think about it for a moment or two; his brows will knit with the effort and then he will decide yes. He will nod and say *All right* and I will say *Deal them then and I'll go and get the teas.* I have my little ways too.

When I get back with the two polystyrene cups of tea, Michael is shouting. In fact, I heard him from the canteen, I heard him as he started. The words he shouts are mostly incomprehensible except for *Bastard!* and *Fucking bastard!* As I approach him I can see his other activity. He bites his wrist. He bites his right wrist, the inside of it, and sometimes, with his left hand, he clutches his balls. *Fucking bastard!* he yells as he draws his wrist away from his mouth. *Fucking bastard!* And he spits on the floor.

Here's your tea, Michael, I say to him, placing his cup before him. Whatever it was that he was in, he snaps out of it immediately. If someone speaks to him, touches his shoulder, he stops shouting. He picks up the tea, sets it carefully to one side. The cards are already dealt and lying in their two piles on the table. He pulls out his packet of cigarettes and takes one out. He doesn't offer me one. He knows. Next week he will have lost this knowledge but over the course of this meeting he has managed to retain it. He tears off the filter tip.

I take a sip of tea and pick up my cards. *OK Michael, let's play.*

Why do you shout, Michael?
I don't know.
Who are you shouting at?
The voices.
What voices?
The voices.
What do they say?
Awful things.
Like what?
Like... like...
Like what?
Terrible things.

How long have you been hearing the voices?
Always.
Always? Not always, Michael. Not when you were a child.
No.
So?
What?
So how long have you been hearing the voices?
Twenty years. Thirty.
Why do you bite your wrist, Michael?
What?
Why do you bite your wrist?
Bite? Bite?
You bite your wrist. Like this. Every time the voices come.
You bite your wrist and you shout. Why do you do it?
I don't know.
Do you know that you do it?
I don't know.

This is not one conversation but the totality of several, spread over months. Getting the answer to a question might take days, the question repeated many times. *Michael, why do you, why do you, why do you, why do you, why do you, why do you, why?*

I don't know.

Soon it is nine–three. I've lied about the hands I've won and managed to get away with it. I've won ten or eleven hands but officially it's nine–three. *Oh Michael,* I say. *Oh Michael.* I shake my head. He looks at me and shrugs.

I begin to lose. I've decided to do it, to let him win. I go for it. It's not as difficult as I thought. In fact it's relatively easy. I thought that maybe if I won by ten hands to six or seven, then that would be OK, less of a rout than usual, but I get to nine–seven and I'm still managing to do it. Nine–eight.

I lose one more hand. That makes six in a row that I've lost and the score is now nine–nine.

You could be on a winner here, Michael, I say.

He looks at me and I try to decipher his expression but I can't. It's his deal. Is he dealing more slowly than usual or am I imagining it?

He discards his eighth card quickly – the jack of hearts. I leave it and take from the pack – five of clubs. This is no good to me so I discard it. Michael picks it up, throws down the ace of diamonds. He spreads his cards on the table – three sevens, the two, three, five of clubs and a joker. He has won the last hand, genuinely won it. The final score is ten–nine. To Michael.

Well, there you go, I say, smiling at him. *There you go.*

He stands up. This is a little unusual as he hasn't yet gathered up the cards. He looks down at me and says, *You threw it away.* He turns and, before I can say anything at all, he is marching towards the door.

I gather up the cards quickly, cursing them as I do so because they are old and greasy and difficult to handle. I ram them into the packet that has been lying all this while beside the metal ashtray. Michael's last cigarette, abandoned some time ago, has burned down to a long, curved stick of ash. Clutching the cards I head for the door.

Michael is already some fifty yards up the street. I can see his spare, shambling figure, his overcoat flapping round him.

Michael! Michael! You forgot your cards.

When I catch up with him I go round in front of him, barring him from the direction he is taking. I put my hands on his shoulders and look at him. There is the usual strong furrow between his eyebrows and I can't tell, even now, even after knowing this man for eighteen months, whether he is angry or unhappy, disappointed, hurt or what. There are no signs to guide me.

I shouldn't have done it, I say. *I shouldn't have done it and I won't do it again. I promise.*

He nods.

I just wanted you to win, you know. Just once. How long have we been playing cards, Michael?

He shrugs, shakes his head.

Eighteen months? Something like that?

He nods, pushes up his lower lip.

In all that time you've never won, Michael. I always win and today I wanted you to win, you know. Just this once.

Taking me completely by surprise, he says, *I won once.*

You did? I'm not so sure about this. Maybe he did win.

Last year. October the seventeenth. Ten–eight.

You did? I'd forgotten.

October the seventeenth. Ten–eight. I won.

I drop my hands from his shoulders. But we stay there, facing each other in silence for a few seconds. I hand him the pack of cards. He takes them, puts them in his pocket, nods.

I'm sorry, Michael, I say.

He pushes his lower lip up again.

Will I see you next week?

He nods.

I'll play fair, Michael, I say. *I'll beat the living shit out of you.*

He smiles.

Well, goodbye then. I put my hand out. He takes it and we shake hands firmly.

I step to one side then and he continues on his way. I watch as he reaches the traffic lights at the top of the road and waits patiently for them to change. The light breeze disturbs the skirts of his coat, the grey towel that depends from his coat pocket. The lights change and he steps out into the road.

Olivia McMahon

ENGLISH AS A FOREIGN LANGUAGE

Lesson 24: Conversation

You're at a party where you've met Jill and Jim. Here are some useful phrases and sentences which will help you to have a conversation with them. Study them and then do the exercises.

Greetings

Good evening/Hello/Hi
I am happy/very happy/pleased/very pleased/delighted to meet you.

Now you introduce yourself to Jill and Jim.

My name is Irfan. I do not want to say you my family name.

Asking questions

In conversation it's useful to be able to ask other people questions about themselves. Here are some questions Jill or Jim might ask you.

What do you do? Where are you from? Are you married? Do you have any children? Do you like it here? How long have you been here?

Now you ask Jill or Jim some questions.

Can you help me? When I will know I can stay in your country? Can you find me doctor who is listening me? Can I go in hostel with peoples from my country?

Answering questions

I am from India/Egypt/Mexico…
I came here a month ago/a year ago – to study English/to work in a bank/in a restaurant. I live in a house/a flat/a guest house

– not far from here/in the centre of town/in Dunbar Street/
Road/Square/Crescent...
I am married/I am not married. I have one, two, three, four ...
children. I have a daughter and a son. I have two daughters
and one son. I have one daughter and two sons. I haven't any
children.

Now tell Jill or Jim about yourself.

*My house is burning. My father is kill. My wife is dead and my
two children is dead. They all shot by soldiers in my village. I
am farmer but they burn my fields also. Now I doing nothing.
I am here since one year. I live in hostel.*

How do you spend your day?

Jill or Jim – a typical day:

I work every day from nine to five. In the evening I usually/often/
sometimes/go to the cinema/a restaurant/the pub.

Now describe your typical day.

*I do not want be here. People here they saying: go home we do
not want you here. Me I want go home but there is no more
home for me. There is no home and no work and no food. In
my country is nothing, nothing. Everybody is dead, my wife,
my children, my father, my friends. Except my mother and I
am frighten she dead also. What I do all day? There is nothing
I can do. Every day is same. I cannot work and I have no
money, not even money to make phone call. I cannot phone if
my mother she is alive. In hostel it is cold and there is only
television I do not understand.*

Expressing emotions

Imagine emotions that Jill or Jim might have expressed to you.

Today I feel happy/excited/over the moon. I've passed my driving
test
I was furious/annoyed/fed up yesterday because I lost at golf

I am worried/anxious/upset that my girlfriend doesn't love me any more

Now tell Jill and Jim about how you are feeling.

I feel frighten. In my country I am torture. My back is hurting still where they are burning it. My kidneys the doctor tell me it will be better but it is not. And I am worry about my mother who is still in my country. I feel I am coward but if I stay I am kill by soldiers. And always I getting upset when I pass butcher's shop because I thinking of soldiers in my village and what they do.

Listener responses

Jill or Jim's responses to what you've been saying might have included the following:

Mmm. Really. Is that so? I see. How nice! How interesting! How exciting! How wonderful! How marvellous! How awful! How terrible!

Now you respond to some of the things they have told you.

I do not understand what you say me.
I do not know why you telling me all this.
I do not know what you talking about.

Concluding the conversation

Well it's been really nice meeting you.
I have enjoyed talking to you.
I hope we meet again some time.

How would you end your conversation with Jill or Jim?

You very nice listen. I hope you able help me. I give you name of hostel. You maybe phone my mother and tell her I still alive. Please, before you go ...

Iain Mac a' Phearsain

AOIS NA LETH-SHÙLA

'Chì an òige an aois,
'S chì an aois am bàs,'
arsa bodach uair,
tac an teine,
ri mion-chànaiche teann
fad air falbh na cheann, mar-thà

'S 'Trobhad ort,'
canaidh mise
ris a' phàiste
am falach fhathast,
ann an tionndadh a h-aodainn,
na h-osnadh-oidhche, na h-anail-latha

'Feuch gun dèan thu fàbhar dhomh,'
canaidh mi ris, no rithse,
''s dualchas eagail is an-fhois,
feirg is fèin-gràine,
a bhristeadh
ann an criomagan suarach cèin:
is dean dìreach na fhreagras ort fhèin,
oir 's e sin an aon rud
a bheireadh faothachadh dhomh fhìn…'

'S an còrr, mar a shaoileadh tu,

fhad 's a chumas mi
aon t-sùil cham air a' bhodach,
thall thairis,
's aon làmh chritheanach,
bhos a seo,
air a broinn mhìn rèidh…
…tighinn thuige

THE ONE-EYED AGE

'Youth sees old age,
And old age sees death,'
said an old fellow once,
by the fire,
to a stuffy ethno-linguist
already wrapped in thought, far away

And, 'Wait a second,'
i'll say,
to the child
still hiding,
in the turning of her face,
in her night-sigh, in her day-breath

'Try and do me a favour,'
i'll say to him, or to her,
'and this heritage of fear and worry
anger and self-loathing,
break it
into insignificant foreign parts:
and do what suits yourself,
for that's the one thing
that would, personally, give me some relief...'

And so on, as you'd imagine,

while i keep
one crooked eye on the old man,
yonder,
and one shaking hand,
over here,
on her flat, smooth stomach...
...still waking

DRÀIBHEAR-TACSI A'S AN EILEAN

Thàinig e gu doras taigh mo sheanmhar,
dràibhear-tacsi bhon cho-op
stais is falt grìosach
à la Elvis, cùl a chinn

'Thill mi,' ars' esan,
air an rathad dhan phort-adhair,
'dà bhliadhn' air ais,'
'Seadh,' arsa mise

'Thill,' ars' esan, 'às a' Bhaile Mhòr,
'eil fhios 'ad,
mi fhìn 's an gille agam
trì bliadhna dh'aois;
bha an t-àite a' dol a dholaidh,
'il fhios 'ad...'
'Seadh,' arsa mise

'Bha e fàs cus dhomh:
drugaichean, gangaichean,
chinks is niggers,
'l fhios 'ad...'

'M'mm,' arsa mise,
a' coimhead
air cùl a chin, à la Elvis,
air an uaireadair agam fhìn,
's a-mach an uinneag
air an t-sneachd gheal ùr, a' laighe
air poll a's a' chlais, taobh a' rathaid

'So, thill mi dhanan Eilean:
tha drugaichean ann, ceart gu leòr,
ach chan eil an còrr –
chan eil fhathast.'

ISLAND TAXI DRIVER

He came to the door of my grandmother's house,
a taxi driver from the co-op,
moustache and greasy hair
à la Elvis, at the back of his head

'Came home,' he said,
on the way to the airport,
'two years ago,'
'Oh yeah,' i said

'Yeah,' he said, 'back from the Big City,
ya know,
me and my boy,
three years old;
the place was goin' to hell,
ya know...'
'Uh-huh,' i said

'It was gettin' too much for me:
drugs, gangs,
chinks 'n niggers,
ya know...'

'M'mm,' i said,
looking
at the back of his head, à la Elvis,
at my own wrist watch,
and out the window
on the fresh white snow, lying
over mud in the gutter, by the side of the road

'So, came home to the Island:
there's drugs, sure enough,
but not the rest –
not yet.'

Michael Malone

A DAUGHTER'S DIARY

Monday

The phone's siren heckled my thoughts,
an electric shock wedging me into the present.
It was Mother. Said she was coming. Said she
would be fit to visit after all. At the weekend.
Six days stretch before me, coloured red
like carpet, minus the cushioning.
Bickered with husband. Then the twins.
Suddenly they were too loud, too clumsy,
too... *there*. Nerves wound tighter
than wicker on a chair. Time to soak,
ease the flare of pain where neck meets shoulder.
From there it will travel at the speed of noise,
through muscle, skirt bone, slide down my forearm
moulder between second and third knuckle
in a rhythm to match piercing of the phone.

Tuesday

'Sweat dreams?' Tim's face close, stagnant breath
easier to ignore than hard flesh pressed against my thigh.
'Thanks for the alarm cock.' I stumble to the toilet,
drunk on fatigue. Shouted in your sleep, he said.
Couldn't make it out, he said. But it was loud, he laughed.
Pain at nest in my skull.
House vacant today as usual.
No company but thought. Thought harasses and chases.
Thought slips in, slides in, shoots in. Thought clothed
in silent screams and teeth.
Housework won't do itself.
Work, work, busy, busy, work, work. Breathing
like a heat-soaked puppy. Forced calm, fists tight.
It's only mother, for fuck's sake!
Boys ape shark's feeding frenzy at suppertime.
Tim's eyes at bedtime. Guilt gagged my reply. I lie
like cooling meat on a marble slab, while Tim
is chased by sweat and hot release, into his dreams.

Wednesday

Tucked away a pill this morning. Seratonin
inserts the right tone in my life. Ribs coated
with the ghost of Pain Barely Remembered. Sleep
a near neighbour last night, each introduction
broken as memories leaked to the surface
like a gloop of oil from the bed of a brackish pond.
Tim read to the boys at bedtime. Usual pattern of limbs
under eider-down. They were all eyes, teeth... casual affection.
Me, cast as observer, peering over the garden fence.
'What's wrong, Love?' Tim's arm harder to shoulder
than his groin. Tried to deflect his thoughts there. With a
squeeze.
'Don't you just want a cuddle?' He moved out of reach.
'Homosexual!' I flee. Cradle my confusion on the couch.
A ceiling apart, for the first time. Arms shelter ribs.
The girl remembers her mother, eyes big, hair everyday electric.
Corded forearms, fingers like bird claws. A mother's fear
she will drop her child. Daughter only allowed shallow breaths.
A mother's fear, she will be to blame for a daughter's brain
skinning the pavement with bone fragments, matter and hair.
Temazepam on the menu tonight, madam.
We have a pill for every occasion.

Thursday

Friday

Soften your gaze; look to one side of your future, you will see in its outline
the shape of your past. On one side I see smoke hanging before a window
breath clears and a girl grips the hem of her mother's trouser, stares while
other children jostle and jump. All cocoon and no play allows Sue to have knees
without blemish, teeth without chips, but fractures the green twig of her psyche.
Went for a swim today. Forgot what the kiss of water felt like full-length on the skin.
This was a daughter's almost daily defiance. If the skin couldn't break
Mother needn't know. What she doesn't know is my jaw muscles
bunched like grapes today. Anger ground against my teeth. Enough.
I've been in the glacial heat of childbirth, for fuck's sake.
Twice, for fuck's sake

Better go. One of the boys has coated the pan (and some of the floor)
in a delightful tan with his supper. Only Mummy's hand can ease
the sand-rub of pain. Illness makes his eyes bigger than Bambi's.
So cute.
Better sleep with Tim tonight. Better groan as well; sound as if
I'm enjoying it.
Then we won't interrupt Mother's sleep with banging bedsprings.
Doubt if she's been 'banged' since Daddy died. Doubt she would know
what it means. Did mother look past the outline of her future
and bandage me against a past she didn't want to repeat?
Ooh, the smell. Vomit's up my nostrils. Better go.

Saturday

Amazing, isn't it? A few well-placed groans.
Actually enjoyed it. Swam in the calm this morning.
Could still feel Tim, moisture amid caress of water.
Mum arrived at suppertime. Boys grabbed
the proffered toys and charged into the street.
Hands wedged into her purple cardigan, she watched them
slide along the path in their new skates.
'Thank you.' My voice hollow.
'You would never have bought me those,'
escaped before I could stop it.
'You were always a little scaredy-cat.'
Her reply hung in the air between us. Burst a bruising.
Something bubbled in my stomach, shone up my throat
and jumped from behind my lips. All eyes locked on me.
'What's so funny?' Mum and Tim echoed.
Another bubble leapt to join the first. More teased open my jaw,
added heat to my cheeks. They were teeming for release.
popping around my ears, paying no heed to Mum's
measured attempt to join in. She, a seal slapping flippers.
Healing tears bounced down my face, evaporated
into the mirth I weaved through the room
dressing the future against the weal of the past.

Andy Manders

BAIRNIE SANG

the loch – still as hell – traps the light
the way a tanner ba's supposetae

there is no right way
tae tell her there's only one moon

or brak what the ripples dae
tae the thing that means mair tae ye

this minute
than the sun

WEE GIRL

she brings me my specs
there ye go
your specs dad

ages pass

with a stick in the sand i show her
ages passing

she brings me life

Lyn Moir

MAPMAKER

Your skin, as usual, is spread over the sheet,
its emptiness a cartographic dream:
your rivers, mountains, boundaries, so clearly
marked last night, have disappeared in sleep.

Mapping pen stiff in unaccustomed hand,
I sketch hesitant lines; once I have drawn
your eyes and coloured them awake, pale ponds
on parchment, my growing skill extends

to hamlets, conurbations, motorways
and their attendant webs. I finalise
the chart with detail so I cannot lose
my bearings, sign it with a compass rose

and navigate the territory, full
of sharp anticipation, lost in thrall
to unexpected cliffs and hidden vales.

Your giant-scale configuration needs
some time to learn, those hastily-drawn roads
which disappear when consciousness intrudes.

NOT EXACTLY A DAVID

You stood in welcome, arms outstretched,
muscled as he was, skin darkened to teak
by years of wind, lacking only patina
from crowds stroking your thighs, feeling
for imperfections in the stone.

You'd weathered well, I thought: scarcely
an ounce of excess fat, still firm
just where you should be. My fingers sensed
no sagging in your flesh, no paper skin,
no ridging blood vessels. I felt

your heartbeat next to mine, could hear
your breathing find my rhythm, knew
for sure you were no statue. We stood
almost unmoving, let heat run through us,
warming our armature of aging bone.

SEA LEOPARD

This morning's sea is groomed, well-manicured,
talons withdrawn when pawing at the shore,

a docile beast lazily outstretched, slow-lapping
the jagged rocks as if aroused from sleep

by thoughts of soft caresses and of food,
its breathing synchronised with rise and fall of tide.

This is the obverse of yesterday's uncontrolled
forays, the animal blood-lusting in the swell,

its features foaming with berserker rage, formation
shot to hell, random attacks spreading confusion,

panic, fear. A schizophrenic character, this sea,
dissimulating power, artfully disguised

as housetrained, bides its time, is playful, lulls
its adversaries while preparing for the kill.

Michael Munro

SNAPSHOT

There you were all the time.
Not ashes nor in heaven,
but in a long-unopened drawer,
star of a one-frame movie
playing in black and white.
The scene
a Brief Encounter train compartment,
rattling down the line to Bray,
your hair much longer, half in shade,
a half-smile for your lad, my father,
your own ghost caught in the window's mirror.
On a forgotten holiday jaunt
my dad snaps the pose
for me to chance on, one nothing day, and
here you are all the time.

Anne B. Murray

GRANDMA'S REVIEW OF *THE BARBER OF SEVILLE*

Well it's a very *modern* version, you know.
Sung in English, you know.
And, there are, you know,
Well, there are, *bedroom scenes,*
That kind of thing,
You know?
BUT, it is Opera.
They keep singing all the time.

Donald S. Murray

A CROFTER'S MARRIAGE

When he approached,
air would crackle
like footsteps across stubble.

When he held her,
skin would bristle
like nettles clutched
within a sheaf of oats.

And she would gather
straws from every quarrel,
raking up old words and looks,
impaling him with fury
wielded like a hay-fork
she twisted nightly
in his side.

Until long aisles of stooks
shadowed their croft,
later to be stored
within that harvest they took home;
stacks darkening their yard.

And then that night the storm set loose
the ropes that lashed
straw down;
unfastening each knot and tie
that bound it in position;
casting aside both stone and driftwood
that held and fixed their labours to the ground.

The next morning,
no wisp or stalk remained;
that swish of wind scythed bare
all legacy of sun and grain
the two of them had shared.

Tracy Patrick

SILENT TRAIN

Now, as I am young
At times I feel the wrath
Of old women's thoughts,
Like when they sit on trains
Next to their husbands
Each watching quietly
Out the window
With nothing to say.
Sometimes they cast a furtive glance
At me sitting opposite
As if curious about the exploits
Of a younger generation and
'It wasn't like that in their day'.
I'd like to tell them,
Phases of life are all alike
Only the frame changes
In the window of time
Buds blossom, bear fruit and die
And I'd like to make it through
To be able to sit quietly
On the train
Next to another elderly
With nothing much to say to each other.

Olive M. Ritch

MAKING TRACKS

'I'd better make tracks,' you'd say
slowly and sincerely before leaving,
taking with you the smell of Lifebuoy soap.

Every week you came
and every week you left. Amused
we watched you cross the fields

with your big tackety-boots and
trousers walloping round your thin legs.
Then you'd come again, promising

to make tracks. Your utterances were laboured
and limited but you tried, baring your teeth
when misunderstood. Some neighbours sighed,

some showed neighbourliness. We did
not understand your difference, the red hair
and bushy eyebrows were not the whole story

but we, young children, were not told.
It was not until you louped
across the fields for the last time

that we found out you were special.
And after the funeral we wondered
if you were in Heaven, making tracks.

TOO BIG FOR HER BOOKS

Her tongue
was different
less coarse, confident
in the subjunctive; exploring
terrain unfurled
by her father's plough,
from neoclassicism
to romanticism; showing off
with sniggers at his split infinitives.
But he did not care
to dress up his words
in their Sunday best;
proud to speak plain
with no fancy furrows
in the landscape. His words
squeezed out between chores
were few and chosen like seedlings
to plant in the dark soil.

Lesley Sargent

AN IGNORANCE OF SOUND

I bumped into the music maker accidentally one summer's afternoon in the countryside.

A tall man in a long, green overcoat, his haversack filled to bulging with clinking sounds. I was inquisitive, unusually unafraid of his strangeness.

'What are you doing?' I asked directly to his spoon-bowl eyes.

'Collecting,' he replied.

I watched him approach a long-stalked dandelion which he skimmed quickly with a jam jar before slipping on the lid.

'Insects?' I pushed.

'No. Sounds,' he corrected.

I was intrigued and continued to watch him for a further half hour as he stalked the long grass like a crane.

'What kind of sounds?' I ventured, as he was about to cork a pretty blue-glass bottle. He frowned at me. 'You've just contaminated the whispering of grass.' He turned the bottle upside down and emptied it into the breeze.

'A person shouldn't speak during these forays,' he said to the horizon. 'The collection must always be pure.'

I apologised. He smiled.

Since there was no objection to my silent presence and I had nothing better to do, I followed him for the rest of the afternoon. I followed him until each of the containers he carried in his haversack had been filled. As he carefully adjusted the straps for comfort he muttered, 'Tea?' I interpreted this as an economical invitation and responded likewise. 'Where?'

He pointed up the hill with a finger stained from sound. We followed its direction. His home was a tiny cottage with two rooms; one for sleeping, eating and living, the other for the storage of his collection. I sipped my tea with sudden nervousness. In the open this man seemed diluted by the air, but within the confines of that small building his presence began to concentrate. I felt overwhelmed by the strangeness of it all. It became too much to believe, so I left.

For several days afterwards I found moments to ponder my new acquaintance. All my silences revealed themselves to be simply an ignorance of sound. Now I could hear the things that before I hadn't listened to. The tiniest of noises: a mouse breathing behind the skirting board, a spider spinning its web, a fly eating the sugar. And yet still I could revert to the silence of before and hear nothing. I switched it on. I switched it off.

On realising my newfound skill I of course rushed to tell. Stumbling over the muddy hoof holes of cows, my meagre torch barely juddered the route into sight. I was disappointed to find he was not at home. Still, this gave me the chance to practice my new talent. Perched on the doorstep I concentrated my hearing until it found his hand brushing his hair from his eyes. I knew he was nearby, down in the woods capturing the sound of mushrooms pushing up through the soil. By the time he got back, he knew that I knew – I had whispered it into my hand. He said nothing, but I heard his heart skip a beat.

That evening he showed me that there is no such thing as silence. That even objects stationary with dust emit a song. He opened jars together and I heard the symphony of rose petals closing on raindrops, ladybirds singing to unfurling bracken fronds, stones communing with the earth. The last small bottle he opened contained a melody sweet with dew in early morning sunshine and when I asked him what it was, he said it was me.

As I left, he offered a jar into my hand. 'For later,' he said.

I keep it safe, out of direct sunlight, with the lid on. One day when he returns, I will let him out.

Andrew Murray Scott

FROM 'VISIONS OF ADHAMHNÁN'

See, they tie you to these fiery pillars
You'll have a sea of molten lava
up to your chin
snakes around your waist,
other people's ordure to breathe.

Huge crowds stand around
in tar pools, forever, like.
No pause, no rest, no conversation.
A little conversation would make it
all okay.

All the time there's striking and arguing
Burning the faces of the wretches
– and fiery rain.
Yes, it is weird.

Streams of fire from every
facial orifice, probably also
nails in your tongue and head.

Too late now.
You must have deserved it –
but all the wailing and lamenting...
that's the real killer.

THE LIGHTS OF LAS CRUCES

Empty flatlines, New Mexico
tundra rolling backwards in the window,
you can see for two days

but as it darkens, fades out,
stars emerge and something else
far off –

nearer, I see a few sad lights:
car headlights exposing a tin shed.

And – get this – a dog is tied to the fender.
Where do they think he's going to run?

And where have they come from anyway
where do they live when there is nothing

nothing, not even a horizon?
Just stars, like chrome-plated rivets,
to bolt-on the corrugated roof.

Frances Sessford

CARING FOR MR LEWIS

He had been brought in overnight and was her only new patient when she had come back on duty. The ward sister had rapped through the day's rota, then had asked her to wait behind while the other staff dispersed.

'There's another patient for your list. I want you to take charge of Mr Lewis. He needs special handling. Make sure you read his case notes.'

He had a bedsore on his hip the size of a man's fist. It had been neglected, the care home only calling in the doctor when the thing was clearly out of control. Her first task that morning was to assess the damage. She stripped away the existing dressing and felt her cereal plunging around in her gut. She'd had to excuse herself. He had apologised when she returned.

'You don't need to apologise, Mr Lewis.' Professional, distant. She was in control.

The other staff avoided him as instructed, dealing with him only when absolutely necessary. She was his only point of contact. The more intimate aspects of his care were dealt with by male auxiliaries. He seemed unperturbed by this ostracism, even seemed to expect it.

He accepted everything, without complaint or argument. Every day he would twist into the correct position for her, then wince in silence while she sluiced the bedsore again and again, packing it tight with fresh dressing and applying the final massive padded bandage. It stuck out like a snowy pom-pom on his bony hip. It looked ridiculous, mirroring the futility of her efforts. It would never heal.

On the third morning he had been reading the paper when she had approached his bed to do the dressing. They both knew the drill by now, him rolling with difficulty into the correct position, while she ripped open packets with professional haste, tipping the contents onto the surface of her scrubbed trolley. He began to comment on the story in the paper while she worked; she grunted small responses, saying as little as she could.

After the dressing she straightened his bed sheets and was about to wheel the trolley away when his paper slipped to the floor, spilling into its separate sheets.

'I'll get it!' She was on her knees, sorting the pages into the correct order before she realised what she was doing. It was automatic.

She liked to try and find the time to do some small kindnesses for her patients. Hospitals were such lonely places. He had none of the nervous bravado of the men, the fussing expectancy of some of the women. He was meek, always obedient, always grateful. Not knowing, she would have thought him a nice man, even a gentleman. In this one unguarded moment she had forgotten the shocking contents of his case notes. By helping him, even in this tiny way, she had colluded, shared his guilt. She had enough of her own.

She scrabbled up with the paper, trying not to touch his hand when she passed it to him.

'There you are.' She hastened away, rattling the trolley in front of her to drown out his thanks.

Has one daughter, the case notes stated, *who remains close to him. Courteous towards staff.* She was bright and tiny, wore a business suit and high heels and had a long swinging ponytail. The first night she came, Steph directed her to where her father was, then gazed after her. She knew this was the patients' private time, knew she should be keeping a low profile but she couldn't help it. She wanted to see how they would greet each other. She wanted to see that bright little bird turn into a spitting virago, bringing the vase and sweets and juice bottles and rails and curtains crashing down around his head, screaming her agony and her shame, making every head turn. Or, perhaps, begin to mutilate him, methodically, deliberately, first the drips, then the bandages, ripping them away to leave him bleeding and crawling, without aid or succour. But they were just like all the other patients and visitors. When he saw her approaching he raised his hand a few inches from his side; she kissed him on the forehead, rearranging his effects on the bedside cabinet before sitting down. Steph watched her unwrapping a bottle of Lucozade and pouring him a tumblerful. She felt betrayed.

A nudge in the small of her back made her turn.

'C'mon, let's get a fag while they're all occupied. Charlie's holding the fort.'

Four of them crowded into the gloomy sluice, fumbling deep in their pockets for Silk Cut and lighters. The window was open wide, showing the city of well people going about their business, going home. They took it in turns to squeeze to the window and peer out, blowing their smoke away. Steph wondered what these mysterious clouds would look like to passers-by, if they would guess the source: four tired, nicotine-starved nurses. Schoolboys would imagine a ghastly furnace belching the vapourised remains of operations, while office workers would hurry past, eyes to the pavement, noses clean. They didn't want to know. The sick frighten them, she thought. They frighten me.

One of them asked the inevitable question, she wasn't sure who, she was gazing out into the summer evening. She turned back to the three expectant shadows close to her, smelling their nicotine breath.

'Well, you know. I just do what I need to then move on to someone else.'

'Reckon that care home just left him to stew. Then we get him to repair the damage.'

'Lucky he got you, Steph. I don't think I could've.'

'You would have,' she said, 'if you'd had to. I don't have much choice, do I?'

'Neither did his daughter. Can't believe she comes to see him. And so pleasant. You'd never know, would you?'

Coos of agreement bounced off the metal surfaces of the sluice. A vortex of leaves rustled below a ventilation shaft in the wall outside. *No, you'd never know.* She tried to shut down her mind.

'Mummy.' She had whispered it to the leaves beneath her.

She had lain breathing in the smell of the damp earth for a long time before she opened her eyes. She kept quiet and still, as the man had told her, when he had promised her ice cream in the life before the wood. She did not know how long it had lasted, the frenzied, nauseating violation. It had just stopped, as suddenly as it had begun, and he had run away. She had not moved from how he had left her, because she did not think that she could. Darkness came down but she felt no terror, only relief. The trees sighed to her and she wanted to sleep. She began to drift, to feel that the trees had taken her up to their tops. The slamming of car doors startled her. She whimpered, awake now and terrified that the man had returned. She tried to squirm deeper into the soily leaves. But when the police dog nuzzled her she had stumbled up on puppet legs, calling out. Her father had lifted her high before bursting with an agony of sobbing relief.

In the hours that followed she had clung to him, eyes wide and fingers in her mouth. She howled when the nurse took her, so much that she choked. A policewoman told her what a brave girl she was and asked questions. She would not take the dolls they tried to give her. She buried her head in his shoulder, her tears soaking into his sweater. She thought of the treetops.

In the next days and weeks, she screamed at the sight of her father, of any man. For years afterwards she screamed if she thought she would be left alone. It was better now. Now, she just couldn't bear to be touched.

When they trooped back from the sluice, Mr Lewis's daughter was waiting to speak to her.

'He's looking much better. I think he's better off away from that home. That horrible thing on his hip. Will it heal, d'you think?'

The eyes were young, not haunted. *You would never know, would you?*

'We're doing what we can.' The stock phrase.

'I'm sure you are. Well, thanks again.'

Steph looked after the jaunty ponytail. She wanted to run after the daughter, to shake her, slap her, scream at her, 'how can you bear it when your father did that to you?' She thought of her own father, of his anguish, the generosity of his love; how she punished him time and again for another man's crime.

On the fourth morning, Mr Lewis had a slight fever. By noon he was worse and by the time Steph went off shift he was burning. The next day the whites of his eyes had developed a yellow tinge. He lay prone, his gaze rolling between the doctor on one side of his bed and the ward sister on the other. Looking on, Steph thought he seemed rat-like, feral. The doctor finished examining him and he and Sister moved up the ward to continue the argument that was brewing. Steph turned to go too, when he called after her.

'Nurse.'

She turned back. Up close she could see the yellow in his eyes beginning to echo in his skin.

'Yes, Mr Lewis?'

'Is there something wrong with me, Nurse?'

'You're running a temperature. That's all.'

He picked at the bedcovers with withered fingers.

'Is my hip going to get better?'

'It's looking better.'

He looked up at her. His eyes were pleading, asking for

more than she could give. She moved away.

She thought about it going home, grinding her head on the window as the bus crawled from stop to stop. She thought of the lies she told.

His condition deteriorated. One night she saw him hold out his hands to his daughter. They were clasped, suppliant, the distended knuckles and veins visible from where Steph watched at the other end of the ward. She knew he was weeping; the daughter sat frozen, with her face towards the floor. Steph saw her leave the ward that night with unbound hair and dead eyes.

Steph tried to think of him as the bogey man, the monster, but as the days wore on he became a surreal figure, almost ridiculous. He was gradually turning orange. The jaundice was spreading from his liver and poisoning his entire system. There was little to be done. He was weak and couldn't eat and the medication was passing straight through a body already exhausted by previous infections. By now his corneas were an angry reddish yellow. They had to put him in the glass-panelled observation room opposite the nurses' station, away from the eyes of the other patients who were becoming upset, or sometimes just curious, at his appearance.

He was caged. When she was on duty and at the desk, all she had to do was raise her eyes to see him. He would look out of the window for hours, sometimes closing his eyes with his face towards it, as if he craved the light. He never wanted the television, or the radio, or his paper now. Often she would look up and he would be gazing dolefully at her, not looking away when their eyes made contact. His eyes were large and brown, drooping with age, but may once have been soulful. In another unguarded moment a few days ago, she speculated that he had probably once been a handsome man. She'd had to rush to the bathroom to vomit.

He had never spoken to her since that fifth morning. He grew weaker, and for three days only the occasional rolling of his bizarre eyes indicated that he was still alive. Steph's sense of duty led her to complete procedures and fulfill all tasks, regardless of the imminence of death. She continued to attend to him, often when he was unconscious.

On the last evening of his life she approached him to dress the bedsore. He appeared to be asleep, but she heard him murmur. His eyes flickered, and she saw with a shock of revulsion that the corneas were almost the same colour as the irises.

He said 'Janice' in the dry whisper of the dying.

'She'll be here soon, Mr Lewis.'

'You've been good to me, Janice.'

Minutes passed and she thought he had slipped away again. Once more, he whispered. 'More than I deserved. Much more...'

She continued to work, sluicing the sore over and over again, sloughing away the dead tissue, packing the gaping hole with bandages that glowed in the light from the window.

He died on the tenth day, about an hour before she came on duty. She found the ward in chaos, the night staff cursing the inconvenience of an early morning death.

'Haven't even done the early drug round,' moaned the charge nurse. 'The houseman's been, the body's done, you'll just have to get it tied up for the porter coming. God knows when that'll be.'

'Who was it?' she asked, but knowing.

'Old Lewis.'

'Has the daughter been told?'

'Yeah. On her way. I'm off. See you.'

'Wait.' The staff nurse whipped round, impatient for rest.

'Did he say anything?' asked Steph.

'Like what?'

'Before he died – was he conscious?'

'No. Out of it. What made you think he'd say anything?'

The other nurse didn't wait for an answer, but turned to run down the steps, already loosening her uniform as she made for the lockers. Steph caught the smirk on her face. They all thought her soft, she knew it – they always thought she did too much for the patients. For him. What choice had she had?

He was in the same small room. The inert mass of him was sheet-bound under a thin blanket. The new morning's light broke over the bed and its white weight.

She wondered where he was. She could never lose the notion that death had some temporal essence; that 8am here would equate to 12 noon or 6pm in death-land, as it would in Paris or New York; while we're sitting down to breakfast the dead are just getting home from work.

She felt a surge of annoyance, strengthening to an anger that made her sway on her feet. She'd had to do everything for him. She was the one that had had to speak to him, fetch for him, endure the whispering of the bitchier nurses, and now they had cleaned, wrapped and finished him off without her being needed at all. What about her? What about her?

And what about his daughter? She would be here soon. They had covered his face already, thoughtless buggers. Not something that would be very nice for her to see. Her anger began to dissolve in the need for duty. She lifted the shroud's hood up and away from the face. In a gesture that was almost tender she lifted his body to her, smoothing the hood flat behind the shoulders and laying him back on the pillow. She found his comb and straightened his hair. He looked peaceful, as if he was only asleep. She tidied the room, brought in a vase of flowers, busied herself doing small kindnesses.

Morelle Smith

IN THE JAZZ CAFÉ

It's just beginning to get dark
and a blackbird sings of spring
in the courtyard of Blackfriars.
The air is still, speckled with night
and the January blackbird
sings of spring.

In the Jazz Café,
Brenda buys a bottle of red wine
and the owner passes us two tumblers
from behind the bar.
Someone sitting at a table opposite
has an earring and dark hair
and smiles to his companions.

We go home in the pebbled dark,
past the Monument,
and the Italian café
and the shopping centre
wind rustling the garbage bags
and throwing paper
and pizza boxes across the road.
The streets are damp and solitary,
warm and windy
for the time of year.

The young man in the Jazz Café
whose smile did not reach my table
reminded me of Jen, with his earring
and his green eyes.
Jen lives in Delmare Street
and to reach his house
I took the pedestrian bridge
that crosses the railway
and gives you a view of the sea.
When I said I'd best be going
he said yes, you'd better.

That was what he said. And then –
'Otherwise I'd keep you here forever.'
I picked up my books and bag.
Put on my jacket
wondering where the words might be
to say – I'd like to change my mind
and stay – and really, it's OK for you
to keep me here forever.

But there's never space for words like that
and so I leave and walk up Delmare Street,
its old stone houses,
gardens in the front, with summer roses
trailing scent and smells of cut grass
mingling with the salt air of the sea
which I catch a glimpse of
when I turn around.

Falling in love with city streets
is a hazard only if you miss
the boundary between the pavement
and the road, dividing line between
protective, tended gardens
and the highways with signs like –
'To the Predator's Path' or –
'Lane of Utter Loneliness' or –
'Last Refuge of the Heart' or –
'There's Still Time to Get Off This Highway'.
Open road or tended garden,
which is the more lethal
of the two?

I made a narrow escape
I tell myself, no mistake about it
as I turn around and there's the grey sea
on horizon and a whiff of salt.
I cross the bridge
over the railway and wake up
in the morning with an ache
between my shoulder blades
as if I had carried something heavy
on my back for a long long time.

I spent the summer
trying to shrug it off,
kept myself busy painting walls
and hanging pictures at the exhibition.
I grew precise and intimate
with folds of muslin, staple guns
and velvet hangings that I stroked
with vague nostalgia I couldn't place
until Jen walked inside one day
and I ran my fingers carelessly
across his head and the soft fur
of his hair reminded me –
of velvet. Not that I had ever touched
his hair before, but I should
have known – I don't know
what exactly but there was this
strong sensation in my fingers
telling me I now knew something
that I should have known before.

Jen takes me two blocks down the street
where we rescue an abandoned chair
and bring it back with us,
to the exhibition.
He has tattoos, one earring,
a sheaf of papers and a ball of stories
that he can't unwind.
He looks at me for clues
and I know I must abandon, now,
my pretence of counsellor, of objectivity,
of older sister who knows
all the answers, for I have none,
just this gesture of my fingers
moving through his hair.

Soon after that, he leaves
and when the exhibition closes
I take the chair home.
As we dismantle velvet, muslin,
nails and the branches, stones,
shells and tapestries and sculptures
from the window,

there is a chill, a shiver
in the grey air, that was
not there before.

It was not there in the early morning
sunshine kissing the flagstones
and the fronts of buildings
when we opened the doors,
spread butter on croissants
and gave coffee and wine to our friends,
and when he came he brought
the salted sea air with him
and pieces of a story he kept trying
to tell me, while I put more coffee
in the filter, poured out cups,
added sugar, handed them out,
spread butter on croissants,
got some on my finger, licked it
and looked at him –

and he said –
'I travelled to Iona' –
'And met an albatross, was that it?'
I spoke crossly, for it was clear
that he'd been stung by miracles
and he kept finding his way back to me,
needing me to hear his story.
'Well, I hope you didn't kill it.'

Me, I was just jealous
and he grinned at me
and I caught pieces of his story,
among the croissant crumbs
and sugar cubes and milk cartons
and wine bottles and the bracelets
of my friends and the bright colours
that they wore and the talk
and the hanging pictures,
glinting in the sunlight
sloping and slinking through the open door.

But when we said goodbye to the
nasturtiums leaning their soft
orange petals on the ledge
outside the window –
goodbye to the downy folds of
muslin on the walls
and the snakes of gold thread in the hangings,
the sky was parcelled up
tight, in its drawstring bag of cloud
and the air snipped its chilly teeth
at us.

I still have the chair we found
abandoned in the street –
I also have phone messages
and cards and promises to meet up –
soon – and – I see someone in the Jazz Café
and I remember
smells of sea and cut grass,
the green eyes, the feel of velvet
as I stroke his hair; crossing the bridge
over the railway line, crossing the threshold,
out into the street –
'You'd better go, otherwise
I'll keep you here forever.'

Falling in love with city streets
and tended gardens
and the scent of roses –
and choosing the highway –
What stays forever anyway?
I say to Brenda, as she
pours more wine and I watch
the young man with the earring
laughing, in the Jazz Café.
'Some memories do, I guess,'
she says.

Yvonne Spence

TEA OR COCOA

I close da bedroom door ahint me tae keep da warmth in for Rose; she feels da cauld something terrible dese days. I go intae da kitchen and fill da kettle. It's a dreich kind a day, and when I fetch in peats there's something aboot da touch o fall in da air dat reminds me o da day I met Rose.

Funny how it still sticks in my mind. I had been hame in Shetland since da simmer o forty-six, having been demobbed early on account o working in da building trade – dey needed all hands tae repair bombed oot buildings. By dat time, in da fall of forty-eight, I wis earning a good wage, and I wis ready tae settle down.

I shared digs in Lerwick wi Bill Peterson. He wis a fine enough bloke, but we both worked for da same firm and sometimes you can have enough of a person. And I'd shared a bed wi him dat week. Da whole jing-bang o us had been working oot at Weisdale, and some were three tae a bed. In dem days we thought naething o it, but like I say, sometimes Bill could get a bit much. When we got back into Lerwick aboot two on dat Saturday afternoon Bill and his friend Alec went aff tae get their half bottles. I said I wis going back tae da digs for a wash.

I spruced myself up, den wrote a letter tae my mother. I liked tae write her every week, tae lat her ken there wis nothing coming at me, after whit happened wi my sister Avril. I wis licking da stamp when I heard Bill and Alec laughing outside. I had a fair idea dey'd had a dram or twa already.

I wis getting my coat on as dey came in.

'Du's surely no going oot noo,' says Bill, taking a step backwards. His bottle wis half empty.

'I'm wanting tae buy a new shirt,' says I. 'My good ane is getting worn.'

'Hae a dram first,' Alec says.

'Da landlady wisna very happy da last time.'

Bill laughed. 'Aye da worrier Jimmy. She'll never leet if Alec gies her a dose o his charm. Eh Alec?'

I picked up da letter and left.

Dat wis da night I first saw her at da Toon Hall dance. I wid maybe never hae noticed her if I hadna bought a shirt aff her dat afternoon. There wis nane of dis self service malarkey back den, and da shirts were all in drawers ahint da counter.

'I'm needing a new dress shirt, fifteen and a half collar,' says I.

She laid half a dozen shirts on da counter. Dey all looked much da sam tae me. 'Dis ane has a self stripe,' she says, picking it up. Her hair wis in da style o da day, in a wave up over her brow, and den coming down near her eye. But unlike most o da lasses, dere wisna a scrap of lipstick or powder on her face. Her cheeks were pink – like her name though I didn't ken dat den. Years after she telt me she'd had her eye on me for a while, but at da time it never dawned on me dat she wis blushing.

So I asked her whit a self stripe wis.

'It's all white,' she says, 'but it's woven in such a way as tae make it look strippet. See.'

I had a look at da shirt tae see whit she meant.

'It's very smart,' she says.

I never wis much of a hand wi clothes, so I took her word for it, and bought it.

'Will you be wearing it tae da dance da night?' she asked when I wis at da door.

'Likely,' says I.

'I'll maybe see you dere,' she says. Sure enough when I managed tae get Bill woken up and alang da road, she wis da first person I noticed, sitting wi a couple of chums, backs against da wall. Da other two wore fancy rig-outs, da skirts held oot wi layers of lace petticoats, but not Rose. Plain face, plain cotton frocks; nae scarlet lips, nae artificial silks. Dat wis my Rose. She could have had da fancy stuff at cost, but she used tae say all dat finery made her feel like a china doll. She wis an ordinary looking lass, da kind nobody would look at twice. Except me. I'd had too much of da other.

Whit is it about getting auld dat maks everything back tae front? I can mind fine da night I met Rose, but I canna mind if it's tea or cocoa she wants.

So I tramp back alang da corridor.

She opens her eyes as I push back da door. Dese days she struggles tae manage a smile. I mind a time, it must be near forty years ago, dat I heard her laughing. I went tae see whit wis so funny. Da baby had thrown food all ower da kitchen, and his three year auld sister wis refusing tae eat her food. And Rose wis in da middle o it, laughing and laughing.

'Janie says da cheese sauce smells like Daddy's old socks,' Rose says, tears streaming doon her face.

Dat wis Rose; in da middle of whit wid have driven another person mad she saw something funny. So after she'd been ill for months, and da doctor said it wis depression, I knew he wis havering.

'The tests for arthritis and thyroid came back negative,' he says. 'There's no evidence of a physical cause.'

'Rose is no da kind of woman tae get depressed,' says I. 'She's aye been full o life.'

'Depression makes folk lethargic, and this dizziness she keeps complaining of would suggest anxiety,' he says. 'A holiday might perk her up. Why don't you visit Janie in Aberdeen?'

'Oh, I dunna ken if Rose is fit for dat,' I says.

'I could give Rose some anti-depressants,' says da doctor, and my blood boiled. 'But I'd like you to try the holiday first. At this stage I think we'll keep our suspicions to ourselves till we see if she comes out of it. Depression is fairly common in women her age. If the holiday doesn't do the trick we'll have another think.'

I kent fine dis holiday idea wis joost filling in time, but I rang Janie anyway.

Another thing I hae no trouble minding is da look on Janie's face when she saw Rose being brought by wheelchair intae da airport. 'I'm joost a bit run doon,' says Rose, patting Janie's arm. 'Dinna du worry, whin I'm had all da iron tablets da doctor gave me I'll be fine.'

Da first week in Aberdeen all Rose wis fit for wis bed. 'What's wrong with Granny?' da bairns asked. 'Why is she still sleeping?'

'She's tired,' Janie says. Then to me she whispers, 'Whit is it?'

God help me, I felt like an auld fool, but I started tae blubber.

'It's okay Dad,' she says, cuddling me, 'Mam's going tae be fine.'

It reminded me of da way Rose cuddled Janie years ago, saying, 'It's okay pet, Grampy's going tae be fine.' Well, dat time we already knew whit wis wrang and dat it wisna going tae be fine, and for all I knew dis wis da same thing.

Just before we left Aberdeen, Janie says, 'You ken you can

come here if anything happens tae Mum.' I think she meant it, but folk says daft things when dey're trying tae make you feel better.

'Nothing's going tae happen,' I says, auld fool dat I am.

'I ken whit a worrier you are,' she says. 'It's one thing you don't have tae worry about.'

She means well, but whit da hell would I find tae do in Aberdeen all day? Janie wid soon get sick o a doddery auld bugger under her feet, and Graham's all right as son-in-laws go, but he has aboot as much interest in carpentry as I do in accounting.

Wis Taits have never been good at being alone. My father went ower da bows of his ship when I wis nine, and my mother wore black da rest of her days. She found a kind of comfort in her Bible but she wouldn't go near anything dat smacked o plea- sure, 'Your faither widna like it,' she'd say if we tried tae cajole her into coming wi wis tae da Sunday School picnics. Wir granny took wis instead. When da war started Ma wanted me tae get work on a farm tae dodge being called up. I wis a boy of fifteen den, an apprentice joiner; I wid have lied aboot my age tae get into da army if I could have, but I stood five feet five den and I'm da same height again now, da inch I gained has gone wi age. So neither Ma nor myself got our way, and I went tae war at eighteen like da other young men.

Things were never good between Ma and my sister Avril, but when da soldiers arrived in Shetland it got worse. Avril wis a pretty girl, da image of Rita Hayworth, and she reckoned wi her looks she could go far. She had been courting Bill Peterson, bit when he wis called up she began going wi da soldiers. Ordinary ones at first, but it wisna long till she wis going wi da officers.

Ma didn't like it. Avril wid be clarting on da war-paint – powder, rouge and lipstick – and Ma would be yelling.

'Du's like some kind o harlot. I wid be ashamed tae be seen like yon. Whit aboot poor Bill? And whitever would dy poor faither say?'

Avril wid stamp her fit and yell, 'Don't du bring my faither into it du auld hypocrite. All du ever did wis bicker and nag at him. So don't go pretending now dat du loved him.' She had a temper dat could match anything my mother threw at her.

'And whit wid du ken about love, du selfish trollop?'

'Hah!' Avril bared her teeth like a snarling dog. 'More than du ever will. My Albert is an officer. We're getting married after da war. We're going tae live in Surrey.'

'A decent man widna wait till da war is over tae marry his lass.'

'He wants tae give me a proper wedding, but, he's going tae Holland soon, so we have tae wait.'

I wis glad tae get away tae da war for some peace.

Rose wis as far from dat two as I could get. I dunna ken whit I would do without her. It's like somebody stuck a knife through my heart and twisted it, watching her lying there, hardly able tae open her eyes.

'Wis it tea or cocoa du wanted?' Den I burst oot greeting. Rose struggles tae push herself up.

'Let me help. Du has tae take it easy. Da doctors have said.'

'Tae take it any easier I'll have tae give up breathing.'

I canna help it, I start blubbering again. I catch sight of something in da mirror, and wonder who dis auld man is dat's gauping at me. I keep forgetting I'm nearly eighty. Da pair of wis are long past wir prime, and ane o wis has tae go first. I had joost always imagined it wid be me.

Rose was nae better when we got back frae Aberdeen, so I sent for da doctor. 'You promised tae send her for tests.' He opened his mouth tae silence me, but I had worked myself up for dis. 'And dunna give me more o dis depression rubbish,' says I. 'If you couldna get oot of bed for weeks on end wid you no be a bit doon in da dumps?' I've never liked shouting at folk, comes of hearing too much of it, and I had tae sit doon when I'd finished.

I expected him tae look shocked, but he joost stood wi his hand under his chin, concentrating. He turned tae Rose and he says, 'Can you remember when you first felt this weakness?'

'It's been a lang while,' she says.

'You had a bad bout of flu at the start of the year didn't you?'

She nodded. 'I've never been right since.'

'I think that might be the key,' he says.

Well, I thought dat wis him saying it wis da flu. I wis livid. 'You don't have da flu for six months, man.'

'I think it could be ME.'

'ME? Dat's yon yuppie flu, is it no? Rose is in her seventies – she canna have yuppie flu.'

But after endless tests dey finally decided there's a good chance it's ME. A good chance – dey give nothing away dese doctors. If it wisna my Rose, I'd never have believed it. I always thought dis yuppie flu wis just an excuse for laziness.

Once we knew whit it wis, she kept questioning da doctor: 'How did I get it? When will I be better?' Always da optimist, Rose. Getting a name for it perked her up, some days she even managed tae go for a walk, telling folk she met, 'I've had dis ME for eight months, but I tink I could be bettering noo.'

When I asked da doctor, he said there's some folk never get better.

Dat's da way it is wi some. Some folk never get over whit ails dem, folk like wir Avril. She's been waiting fifty years for her soldier, and she's still waiting. Last week Rose sent me intae Lerwick tae buy a book about ME, and I stopped alang da home on my way back.

'Oh Jimmy, it is dat fine tae see de,' Avril says. 'I'm dat pleased du's got back from Germany okay. Has du brought my Albert wi de?'

Some days I try tae get her tae speak sense, but dat day I couldn't face it. God help me, I just turned me aboot and left. Da irony of it is Bill Peterson is in da same home. He had a stroke a few years syne, and never got back on form. He never married, though there's plenty would have had him. I heard a story dat he had a girl in Belguim who got killed. I never liked tae ask him. Dey coulda been companions, Avril and him, but neither of dem has a clue.

Still, Rose wis fair pleased wi her book. She wanted me tae get her other anes, saying dis illness hasna got her licked yet. It's nearly worn me oot, trekking intae Lerwick for books. Sometimes I worry dat all dis reading will put a strain on her eyes and set her back, but she says as long as she has rests it's okay.

And she says she's had her rest for dis morning, so I prop her up wi some pillows. I pass her da latest book – *Alternative Therapies for ME*. When I go oot tae make da drinks Rose is sitting up wi her head in da book. I'm getting da cups oot when I realise I never found oot whit she wants. She's still sitting up when I go back into da room, and she's got her feet oot ower da bed.

'Dis book says aromatherapy can help,' she says. 'I thought

du could take me intae Lerwick tae yon Complementary Health Clinic.' She slides her feet onto da floor. 'Could du give me a hand getting dressed?'

I take some clothes oot of da drawers: underwear, tights, socks, trousers, jumper, cardigan. We need tae keep her warm. I help her wi her bra, fastening da hooks at da back. Da trousers have an elastic waist, so she manages dem herself, but da effort leaves her exhausted. I help her wi her blouse.

'It says yon aromatherapy stimulates da nervous system and encourages da body tae heal itself,' she says. 'It'll have me right as rain in nae time.'

I'm not sure how tae tell her she might never get better, so I say nothing and pull da jumper ower her head. When her face reappears she points. 'See, da book says I should drink herbal tisanes so I winna be putting any more poisons intae my body tae interfere wi da healing process. I thought we could maybe get some of dem when we're in Lerwick.'

We've got her dressed now, and I help her tae stand up. We shuffle intae da sitting room and she sits by da fire getting her breath back.

'We'll better hae something afore we go,' I say. 'Wis it tea or cocoa du wanted?'

Gary Steven

BAR WORK

I woke up wi the worst hangover I've ever had in my puff. My head was killin me. So I closed my eyes an tried to get back to sleep but pretty soon I had them open again an I noticed all this fuckin blood over my bed. It obviously wisny a hangover. I had two pints last night. An the Guinness isny usually that bad. Mibbe I'd crawled my way home after a hit an run accident or somethin. I definitely hadn't refused to employ any Italian-American film actors lately. My hands an feet were fuckin killin me as well as the head. I looked down at them in amongst aw the blood. I'm tellin you I've never been so shit scared before. Holes aw over me. Feet, legs, fuckin head an hands an shit. One even on the side a my stomach as well. I was meant to start work at the restaurant at half eight too. It's bad enough bein late wi a hangover when you've to choose between breakfast an a shower. But the fuckin stigmata on a Monday mornin, that's just takin the fuckin piss.

I got up. I couldny go inty work lookin like this. They give you a bollockin for a wee bit a stubble or a tattoo. I don't know what they would be like if I turned up wi aw that blood drippin off me. I had to have a shower. Didny feel much like eatin anyway. So I washed. Then I tried to stop the blood pourin out. I shoved a cotton wool ball inty each hole in my feet an wrists, shoved them in tight. Very absorbent them by the way. I pulled the trousers up after that an then wrapped some toilet paper round my feet an put socks an shoes on. The good fuckin shoes an aw. The hands an head I wisny sure about. I went to the kitchen an grabbed this pair a pink rubber gloves. I cut off the wrists an slipped them over the cotton wool balls to stop any leakage. A bit a maskin tape round the edges held them in place. I grabbed a dish clout an rammed it inty the spear wound in my side. Half a roll a the maskin tape around my waist stuck that on. I put my shirt on.

I still had to do somethin about the head, people could see that much easier. I didn't want to walk about scarin weans an stuff. Took me fuckin ages to find a set a filthy old adidas sweatbands. Fuckin perfect disguise. One on each wrist over the pink rubber an one on the nut. That was me set but I'd no chance a makin it on time. If ever I had a decent excuse though, surely the miraculous appearance a the wounds a christ on my person was it. Fuck knows wi this lot I'm workin for the now. You break your leg out waitin tables an they drive you to the vicky for a splint an bring you back in time to finish your shift. I left the house late.

Bus driver never noticed a fuckin thing. I got there, only twenty minutes late. Ten to nine in the mornin an he says to me, 'Evenin Tommy.' I felt like fuckin hookin him but that widny a done my wrists any good at all. Still fuckin hurtin me.

I had hoped it might clear up by lunchtime but it didny look like that was happenin. The boss asked me, 'What's wi the bloody headband, Tommy?' The bastard had the cheek to tell me it didny fit in wi the fuckin uniform. If the fuckin Romans hadny been so good at drawin out a slow death; aimin nails through people an missin all major bones an arteries, I'd a been fucked already an he's complainin about the fuckin colour scheme. So I told him, 'I'm fuckin sweatin blood in this job as usual. That's aw it is.' But then I thought fuck it. 'Well actually I'll tell you fuckin exactly what it is. I woke up wi the fuckin stigmata this mornin. Can you no tell a fuckin miracle when it walks in on bloodied feet to do a shift in the bar ay an Italian restaurant wi ye? Fuck's sake.' The blood was runnin down inty my eyes an everythin. Fuck knows how I was goany get through the shift.

There was aw that cryptosporidium shite in the water an aw so I had extra work to do wi pots an pans an ice buckets full a bottled water instead a usin the taps. An then fuck, that shower I had; 'Don't wash open wounds in tapwater,' they said. Bastard. Probably hoachin wi that wee bastard parasite. Crawlin about inside me, thousands a them. I was the fuckin walkin definition a open fuckin wounds, the religious icon a open wounds, fuckin miracle boy getting eaten up fae the inside out by wee cryptosporidium parashites.

An then I remembered they cotton wool balls in my wrists. How fuckin soggy were they when I pulled them out? It was just in time for my break so I nipped into the toilet. Spent my whole fuckin break cleanin blood off my hands an feet an head. I took the dishcloth out an stole one a their linen napkins to tie round my waist an cover that fucked up gapin hole in my side. They fuckin hate me usin their linen even just for polishin glasses. Their fuckin glasses, I don't give a fuck. I'll serve dirty glasses if they want. I was moppin up blood from a thousand thorny

holes in my heid an then fittin the cloth in under my workshirt.
I came out an they all thought I'd gained weight durin my
break. But how the fuck could I gain weight. If I never had a
fuckin chance to eat anythin. Fuckin fourteen hour shift, wi the
stigmata givin your innards a bit a fresh air an no so much as a
penne arrabiata for your dinner.

An the first thing they did when I got back from my break
was to send me up the stairs to the store for a couple a cases a
tomatoes. I went up the stairs. Walkin was bad enough but
climbin stairs, jesus christ. An I lifted two 18 kilo cases. I lifted
them an the blood started pissin out the holes. But I thought
fuck it, I'll tell them one a the tins up in the stores burst. It's just
tomatoes chef, pomodoro, pomodoro. Nae bother. Fuckin
blood a the lord I should tell the bastards. Thirty six kilos a
fuckin tomatoes. I ended up restin them on my side an of course
that was right on another of my new fuckin orifices so the blood
came pishin out a there as well. I walked inty the kitchen fuckin
dazed an dizzy, dropped the boxes on my bastard feet an set the
blood oozin out between the laces a my shoes. The chef was
like, 'Fuck's sake Tommy, what's up wi you?'

An that was it you know. I was like, 'Fuck's sake. I fuckin
told yous all it's the fuckin stigmata. I'm bleedin fae about
sixty million different holes in my body. An none a them were
there when I went to my bed last night. Jesus fuckin christ!' I
really need to get outa this fuckin job man. I mean you walk
inty work late one day because you've got five or six new holes
in your body, out a which is pourin the blood a christ. An not
only do they complain about you bein late they send you
upstairs to grab a couple a cases a peeled fuckin Italian tomatoes. An then the bastard chef shouts at me. 'Well get out the
fuckin kitchen then, you're makin a mess. I've got to cook in
here.' Could they no at least have asked if I was awright or
anythin? I need to get out a this job, the managers are arse-
holes. I fuckin hate bar work.

Mike Stocks

PIANO STOOL IN TOLLCROSS

Sometimes the minor gods put on a show,
like when we lugged your piano stool across
that mean old Friday nighter in Tollcross,
and you remembered we'd been running low

on contraception since two weeks ago,
and passing Woollies (open until ten
and very cheap on Durex) in we went,
hand in handle with your stool in tow,

and umm-ed and aah-ed the condoms thoughtfully,
while a guard who'd seen most things before
subjected us to extra scrutiny

and conjured up this vision – you, and me,
cavorting with our purchase from that store –
and wondered what the piano stool was for.

PRINCES STREET GARDENS

A dog with one leg missing sniffed a trail
across the park that shadows Princes Street,
and as I thought about his three small feet
I saw a blackbird with a mangled tail.

A flightless bird, a dog that couldn't run—
and neither thinking why, nor knowing more,
and not the dog and not the blackbird saw
my damaged human being looking on.

Count all the crimes for which there's no forgiving,
each forest felled, ten thousand species lost,
the violence done and now the coming cost,

but nature is the cruel conformist place,
and only the human world allots a space
in which the broken beasts can scratch a living.

Alison Swinfen

A PREGNANT PAUSE

And which month
is this in the
silence between us?
Is it sickness I'm
feeling or the form
of a foot?

In the loading of
meaning onto
lids and long fingers
no word soothes the spine,
there's no rhyme
telling time.

Truth is ungainly. It's
fertile and brooding,
warming the words
that are better cold-stored.

So touch me and
tell me of being and
becoming. Feed me coal
for cravings, and
then stamp out the fire.

JAM

And we get jam
with our daily bread.
Stained picking fingers
all sticky with sugar.
Red,
on our bread
and we are fed.

And it's all in your time
for we cannot rush
the dough rising,
or the setting and cooling.
All there and complete
as we spread sticky red
on our bread
and are fed.

Judith Taylor

LAND O' THE FREE

I left my bunnet an hackle in the cage
an went oot wi the wee burd on my heid.
Whit,
nae mair salutin?
spiers the major.
Naw
nae mair salutin
the wee bird telt him.
Aw, aa richt.
But pardon me, I thocht there wis salutin
the major says. *Am I wrang?*

Ach, ye're pardont. Onybody can mak a mistake
the wee burd sang.

(Quartier libre by Jacques Prevert)

Sheila Templeton

HOT CHICK

Ma man sez
'Yer ... HOT.'
Ah sez 'Mmm'
in his ear.
He sez 'Naw
yer HOT, ah mean
sizzlin', hen, ah
could fry an egg
oan yer back.
Whit's wrang,
ur ye no weel?
It's no verra comfy
fur me.
Yerr like a toasty
hot water bottle
a' the time.
Iz this whit thon
Germaine Greer
cries the Change?
Ur you huvven
a hot flush?'

'Naw,' ah sez,
'ah'm huvven
a Power Surge.
An' you kin sleep
on the flerr.'

Fiona Ritchie Walker

TWEAK

This is her word, that baby bird mouth
makes it her own, that slender voice
sends it flying. Everything she touches
needs a final tweak, crimson nails
pincer stray hairs into place,
pull strands of fringe to perfection.

She tweaks in the mirror.
I catch it on the rebound, feel
it hit the back of my throat,
trickle down. Her fingers
are teasing my feathered edges,
gliding over my double crown.

Tweak slides down through my stomach,
gathers speed, grows its own wings.

138

Luke Williams

QUESTIONS, I
Evie asks herself some questions

Who are you?
My name is Evie Steppman.
Where were you born?
Children's Hospital, Lagos.
When?
1947.
In any special circumstance?
I was late.
How late?
Two months.
Go on.
Not all children grow by the clock. I, for one, was not ready to
emerge after the allotted time. Happy in the womb, unaffected
by the laws of substance, I felt no hurry to budge. I possessed
the foetal license – indeed, the prerogative – to moot and
gambol. Trembles met with, 'Do you feel him kick, dear?' or,
'Certainly a strong one.' Hands and ears and whispering lips
were pressed to my mother's stomach. 'It's like a factory in
there,' joked my father, 'I can hear clattering machinery, a
baby-building works.' I delighted in my formlessness. Half fish,
half girl – a mermaid. I tumbled free from gravity. I luxuriated
in the confusion of it all. Such licensed disorder!

[Pause]

How did your belated arrival affect your life?
It killed my mother.
Yes.
It caused my father to lose his faith in Progress.
Yes.
It gave me the power of listening.
How so?
In the evenings, when each day's duty as District Officer for
Lagos was complete, my father crouched beside my mother and
chattered to her bulging belly. He was a second son, lesser both
in age and strength than his brawny brother. He received no
inheritance. And so my father fought back with the only weapon

he knew: Learning. Kneeling awkwardly on the veranda floor, his hands gripping the chaise longue upon which Mother lay, he read me Dickens and Darwin, Typhoon and Treasure Island. He recited Housman and the Lord's Prayer. I learned how the elephant got his trunk, the principles of Indirect Rule. I entered with Al-Idrisi into the distant corridors of his geography. We accompanied Mungo Park east along the Niger and, with Sir Frederic Lugard, sojourned at Lokaja. He discoursed on zoos and craniology. He told of masks, of goblins, turning blithely from myth to biology to Christmas. One evening, as he attended to the names of the seven seas, in between the Indian and the Aegean, I punched him on the nose. Undeterred, he opened the Bible and related the seven sins. While I turned somersaults and figures-of-eight, Father worked through the volumes that informed his inconsistent mind.

And perhaps it was the monotony of this daily address (accompanied by the tic-toc of Father's pocket watch, which invariably slipped from its niche to rest – an inverse stethoscope – on Mother's belly) that bred in me the will to listen. He spoke in the most formal and stilted manner, as if I was a schoolboy!, his voice bright and always earnest. Each history, novel, treatise, sounded to my fragile ear as if rendered from stone. In this way I found it hard to distinguish H. Rider Haggard from Aunt Phoebe's letters, the Great Chain of Being from the Nocturama at Edinburgh Zoo. Be it lecture or tall tale, each was delivered in Father's reading voice.

Week after week he persisted with this schooling. I felt the discomfort of one who hears a long and badly told joke. Setting out to tell a story, which may have been a fine one, Father invariably failed. The world he brought me via my mother's stomach was a colourful place, but devoid of nuance, a world in which every legend and report, every plot and character appeared alike.

How strange it was, then, to find, in the outside world, contrast, division, *difference*. Inside my mother, I knew that out there a giant space existed, a territory far greater than our little home allowed. Already my ears had started to pick out sounds from the amorphous hum of Lagos. I recognised, for instance, the whisper of the sea. This was easy, for I grew in moon cycles. I perceived the sharp salute of gunfire and the chimes of Lagos Clock. These sounds I feared. Yet these scattered tones were engulfed in the coursing hum of blood, soothing to my ear, and

by my father's nightly readings. It was to be much later that I
perfected my art of listening.

[Pause]

You dallied in the womb because you were afraid of the outside?
I was comfy.

You were hungry for his knowledge?
I never wholly got it. Father was endlessly pedantic and erratic.
A whim might catch him and take us on an alternate inquiry. He
would abandon his station beside Mother and go cycling,
returning days later only to begin elsewhere. Quite simply: my
father never finished a single lesson. Can you see what this did
to me, a mere unborn? Just as he was reaching the climax of his
recitation, his mind failed, he wandered from the current theme,
anxious to pursue the next.

Did you enjoy your father's readings?
They wearied me. He gave me lessons and I wanted stories. But
I listened. With frustration I listened. And as I did my ears began
to develop. The more I heard, the greater and more esoteric my
knowledge became, the keener my powers of listening. There's
no chance for other senses to refine themselves in the womb, for
what can you see inside a silky space-chamber? The amniotic
fluid – salty, viscous and vile – is the only flavour. And what to
smell?

[Pause]

Tell me about your powers of listening.
I am losing them. Slowly at first, but with increasing alacrity,
the sounds that I once so clearly perceived are starting to
merge into clamour. No longer can I distinguish, sort and
order each little noise. It is true, my hearing is still uncom-
monly acute. With effort I can pick out echoes from the hustle-
bustle of my childhood in Lagos. Seated uncomfortably in my
wicker swinging-basket, suspended above our immaculate
lawn which sloped toward the bay, I hear the calls of Jankara
market women, broadcasting the succulence of their commodi-
ties in myriad vernaculars, so that amidst the commonality of
staple foods – palm oil, tilapia, yams, groundnuts and spices –

I imagine I hear entreaties to enter card games, river cruises, witch hunts. The elephant grass at the edge of our garden obscures my view of Ade – our servant-boy – but I can hear him; he is making telephones from empty cans and lengths of string. In the distance the thud of leather striking willow tells me that Captain Macaulty has scored another 4. I hear teacups, Father playing solitaire, clocks, footsteps, the bulb-horn of a goods lorry; listening harder, I hear the sound of the driver's forehead pressed against the windscreen, vibrating in time to the engine idling. In the harbour, below the mastheads, there is the clamour of men unloading soap, pots and pans, mail, saddles, an umbrella, tea, sugar, gin, boxes of cigars, rifles, tuxedos, steel, fireworks, brine, chocolate, camp-chairs, and an elegant high-sprung dogcart made in Manchester. I hear the cries of merchant seamen and they commingle in my mind with older, less familiar voices; those of the first English explorers, the unfortunate men who, not two hundred years ago, sang the most sinister of sea shanties as they neared the Niger coast:

> *Beware and take care of the Bight of Benin*
> *There's one comes out for forty goes in;*

and those of the slaving ships, their silent crewmen, and the barely audible dirge of their living cargo. All these sounds I hear, as if before me.

Yet there are disturbing lapses in my audition. I find for instance I cannot play my favourite childhood game. During the long hot hours after lunch, when Father was taking his afternoon nap, and Ben – our cook, Ade's father – was preparing dinner, I would slip from my bedroom and into the streets of Lagos. I recall the brightness. The smell of sweating bodies, drying fish and open sewers. Concealed between the flagpoles at Tinubu Square, I would close my eyes. Amid the strangely intelligible street-sounds – by my eighth year I had distinguished between the pitch of the Governor's Austin 12 Tourer and the Chief's Mercedes – I detected other noises, new to my ears; noises that disturbed and delighted; noises that appeared to a maturing girl at once violent and inspired. Back home I would play out the drama of these stolen moments with my little dolls. I had Red Ridinghood kissing Paddington Bear, my Victorian china doll groping with the Nigger Minstrel from

America. And if now I can only describe these sounds in insipid terms, it simply proves the inadequacy of my failing memory.

Still worse: I find I can no longer listen to neighbourly chit-chat; as if, in my middle years, I am turning into the vacant, fidgety child I never was. Where once I possessed the power to listen, I now squirm, empathise and feel compelled to interject. How different it was then! I grew, developed like any child. I began to see, to touch, to smell and taste. But before it all I learnt to listen. It was this still quality, this gift for rapt attention, that made me the darling of the African imperial. Admittedly, there were questions. Tranquillity and soft examination – a combination irresistible to the men and women of British Africa. You see, the architects of empire were a muddled bunch: second sons, bored wives, athletes, soldiers, clergy. They each had something to prove, to boast about...*to confess.* 'Why did you come to Africa?' – none knew precisely, but everyone had a story – 'How I got here? Well...' 'Those pesky clerks!' 'I love to shoot monkeys.' Unlike my father's stern address, these stories were alive, they changed and evolved, they gathered elements from disparate places, over- and inter-lapping.

And I, Evie Steppman, heard them all. I am the (until now silent) repository of the dreamers of empire.
Why did you put up with it?
Simple: I found in these confessions the stories that were bluntly absent from Father's lessons.

[Pause. A scurrying among the rafters.]

It is these same stories that I am now forgetting.
What are you going to do?
I must write. Set down on paper. Faithfully record my past before it rises to a tinnitus and recedes from memory. But how dreary. How dim and unnatural words are! How distanced from the live thing, the unknown generous gentlemanly thing, the cutting and distorting yet strangely exact pitch of my child's hearing, are words. There are no words that can transcribe the vibrancy of my audition.

Reluctantly I write.

[Pause. Silence. From which opens quiet sea-sounds, dully, distantly, echoes of surf purl, rockwhirl, seawrecks, tin-can music. Silence. Through which rasps a shrill whistle, a dog's

bark, softcrunching boots. Silence. And now wakings of civil-
isations, battles, seagulfs, sirens.]

What time is it now?
Early 2002.
Where are you?
Gullane, East Scotland.
From where, exactly, are you writing?
From the house that we – Ben, Father, Mr Rafferty and I –
lived in from October 1960.
Tell me about this house.
It is a two storey villa on the seafront, designed with Victorian
furore, fuelled by cash and images of Britain abroad. I have
confined myself to the ground floor, though of late I have made
frequent trips to the attic, which I am attempting to clear out.
What, may I ask, is there to expunge?
A machete, a Lord's lamp, intricate carved ivory, a box marked
'Uncommon Things'. There is a silver pocket watch with an
absent minute hand. A Gunn and Moore cricket bat. A phono-
graph. Hanging by a single hook is a map-of-the-world, great
gaps bitten from it. Books line the west-facing wall: histories,
novels, treatises, a set of Encyclopaedia Britannica, 1911. But
most of all, dominating the room, are my father's men's magazines, the entire *Playboy* catalogue from October 1960 to
May 1976 – being the month he could no longer turn pounds
into pink ladies. He quit his glossy monthly and, with it, his
last link to the wider world. It was also at this time his mind
became riddled by Cat.
Cat?
Back in Britain Father sank deeper and impenetrably into his
past. Spending more and more hours in the attic, listless with
memories of a glorious career, he receded into the incongruous
corridors of History. Time was stalking him like a shadow cat.
During his great top-floor retreat (he descended only to pass
water, and, latterly, not at all, pissing in a metal pail), he
bewailed the scratching noise – mice? – resounding about him.
Even now, writing these words from my own station in the attic,
I can follow the sound of tiny feet up beyond the ceiling, and
across, left, right, to the oak-wood walls; yes, the scratching is
all about me, the mice are in the attic, making homes among the
discarded items of Father's addled mind.
　　The thing about the attic is that you can hear every move-

ment, any little noise a body might make. Just as now, after dark, I report the scurry of mice, I recognise other sounds. Sounds from an impending past. Sounds echoing loud in my head so that sometimes I am unable to distinguish between the mice and the hubbub of my recalling. Weeks, months, decades, are ringing in my ears. Births and deaths, salt water and fixed cricket matches are crying for attention. I hear cooks, continents and stubborn stains. There are bats too, and sparrows. Small life my attic sustains.

Though equally my attic bears objects inanimate. Once-life. Like the old trunk full with Mother's clothes, unused and not useful, smelling of naphthalene.

But what of Cat?

Let me tell you a story. When S. was aged eight he saw a sheep hanging in a butcher's window. S. told his father because he was hungry and hadn't eaten meat in months.

'Go, buy me the head of the sheep!' his father commanded.

S. went to the butcher and bought the head. But on the way home he ate the meat and returned with a skull.

'What have you brought me?' his father cried.

'It's a sheep's head,' S. said.

'Where are the eyes?'

'The sheep was blind.'

'And where's the tongue?'

'The sheep was dumb.'

'And where are the ears?'

'The sheep was deaf.'

'*Cat*,' cried his father. But S. had already run to the forest, leaving scorch marks on the dirt road.

...but I tell too much.

Go on.

[Pause]

Tell me more.

[Silence]

You can't stop there.

[Pause. Silence. A cat's cry. A scratching of sharpclawing paws. A winged insect thunders against the skylight.]

Picture this: A woman, not young, sits at her makeshift desk; ponderously, with shaky hands, for it is cold, she scans the room; her eyes rest first on the keys of her computer, then rise to the skylight, taking in the darkening sky; she hears the noise of the traffic; slowly, eschewing the city-sounds below, she turns from the skylight, rubbing her palms together for warmth, and begins – where to begin? – to recount her life – which is really the lives of her and Ben and her father, the impossibility of a mother who died in childbirth and the lives of countless others – and what to tell? – what is true, what was once true, what has been, might be, is? – and how to go about it? She asks herself a question – *Who are you?* – and another – *Where were you born?* – because this is what she knows best – at the outset, in the middle, she always asked questions; and here come the words, bit-by-bit; bit-by-bit the words form upon the page...

Jim C. Wilson

GOODBYE

The removal van is standing in your drive.
As I pass by, your daughter smiles and waves;
she remembers me. She remembers me
with you. And you're about to leave – I guess.

So I work hard in my garden, gathering
dead holly leaves, just a brief walk away
from where the massive van is standing, white
as an iceberg, ominous as a hearse.

The springtime sun is almost hot. Each time
I rest, I look, until I see the van
is moving, turning, going. Just sunlight
now on an empty street, your empty drive.

I work on as the shadows grow, packing leaves
of green, of brown, deep into a refuse bag,
wondering about that unsaid word, aware
of the stinging, the newest drops of blood.

THINGS THAT MATTER

The things that really matter,
a famous Irish poet said,
are casual, insignificant...
Like the way your eyes are
no colour I know; how your back
seems stiff, yet I'd sing out loud
to praise it; how your arm
touches mine, just by chance,
perhaps; how you answer
each letter immediately.
These things, and more, will
never be News but, each day,
are enough for rejoicing.

Jonathan Wonham

DON'T FORGET

Don't forget those dreams.
Don't forget the last train, the first train,
'swaying through the night'.
Don't forget the writing on your foot
or the words she taught you in bed.

Don't forget the night of scarves,
the seduction on the bridge.
Don't forget the constrictions
of her car, or the party
she smashed eggs on your head.

Don't forget the smell of her,
her fists banging on the wall.
Don't forget how you could not forget her
and how you cried on the last train home.
Or was it the first train?

EVENING TRAINS

Let's go over and sit on the sewer
and watch the trains rattle over the points.
Your name is unpronounceable
and nobody knows where I come from.

We should kiss and stay strangers,
performing for the passengers
in their waxy compartments.
Once, I saw a man take off his shoe

and break the window of an evening train.
The cold wind rushed in at him,
pushing him across the carriage
like a convict escaping his cell.

The man was drunk. He cowered down
while the wind whipped over him,
lifting the shirt up his back
and exposing his shining scars.

BIOGRAPHIES

James Aitchison was born in Stirlingshire and educated at the universities of Glasgow and Strathclyde. He has published five collections of poetry and the critical study *The Golden Harvester: The Vision of Edwin Muir*. He now lives with his wife in Gloucestershire.

Liam Murray Bell was born on the Orkney Islands in 1985. He was brought up in Glasgow and educated at Hyndland Secondary School. He is currently in his first year at Glasgow University studying English Literature. *The First Day of Christmas*, written in his sixth year at Hyndland, is his first publication.

Neil Cocker was born in Falkirk in 1972. *Milking the Haggis* is an extract from a novel in progress; another extract was previously published in *Original Sins* (Canongate Prize anthology 2001). A former member of Stirling Writers Group, Neil now lives in Amsterdam, where he works for a whisky company.

Linda Cracknell's short stories have been anthologised and broadcast, and a collection, *Life Drawing*, was published in 2000. She has also written radio drama and is currently working on a first novel. She is currently writer in residence at Brownsbank Cottage, Hugh MacDiarmid's final home, just outside Biggar.

David Cunningham was born in Ayrshire and educated at Glasgow University. His short stories have appeared in various magazines and anthologies. A couple have also been broadcast on BBC Radio. His first novel was recently accepted for publication by Faber & Faber.

Raised in Lincolnshire from the age of eight, Irish poet and singer-songwriter **Mike Dillon** has lived in Edinburgh since the mid-seventies. Winner of the Edinburgh Folksong Competition, he performs his material on a regular basis and his poetry has been published in numerous magazines and in two solo collections.

Angus Dunn: fiction published in *Macallan Shorts*, *New Writing Scotland*, West Highland Free Press etc.; also broadcast on Radio

4, Radio Scotland & Ullapool FM. Poetry has been published here and also there. Winner of Neil Gunn competition 2001, RLS Award 1995. Lives on the Black Isle and works with wood.

Alexis Ferguson was 21 this year, and lives in Glasgow. She is studying for her MA English Literature with Psychology at Glasgow University. Her spare time, if she has any left, is spent writing, and practicing Pipe Band snare drumming in her wee green hut on a hill at Carbeth.

Rody Gorman was born in Dublin and now lives in Skye. His poetry collections include *Fax and Other Poems*; *Cùis-Ghaoil*; *Bealach Garbh*; *Air a' Charbad fo Thalamh/On the Underground* and *Naomhóga na Laoi*. The forthcoming collections *Taaaaaadhaaaaaaal!* and *Tóithín ag Tláithínteacht* will appear in 2004.

Originally from Baillieston, Glasgow, **Charlie Gracie** now lives with his family in Thornhill near Stirling. He has had poetry and short stories in a number of publications in the last three years, including *Cutting Teeth*, *Pushing Out The Boat*, *Poetry Scotland* and *New Writing Scotland 19* and *20*. His work is generally about green places and what lies beyond the surface, and about dark places and the glimmer that lives there.

Stephanie Green: born in Sussex. Educated at Trinity College, Dublin and Kent University. Publications include a novel, *The Triple Spiral*, (Walker Books, 1989) and some poems in literary magazines, including *NorthWords*. She has lived in Edinburgh since 1999 and is currently on the MPhil course in Creative Writing at Glasgow University.

Jen Hadfield graduated from Glasgow and Strathclyde's MLitt in Creative Writing in 2001, and used a Scottish Arts Council bursary in 2002 to travel to Shetland and Skye and write a poetry collection. The manuscript, *Lorelei's Lore*, received an Eric Gregory Award in 2003. Her website is at **www.rogueseeds.co.uk**

Paul De Havilland lives in Leith, and makes a living teaching Project Management and IT. *Widow* is his second published story. Current writing projects include the inevitable novel, and a children's story.

Linda Henderson has completed her first novel, *Soul Diving*, and continues to write poetry and short stories. She has published in *North Words*, *Poetry Scotland*, *PocketBooks (Football Haiku)* and *Island*. A short story was included in *Word Jig: New Fiction from Scotland* (New York 2003). She lives on Skye.

Brent Hodgson's work has been published widely in literary magazines and anthologies. Pamphlets of his poetry have been published by Corbie Press, *Markings* special editions and Kettilonia. Recent work has appeared in *Islands*, *Lallans*, *Chapman*, *Omega* and the Itchy Coo publication *King of the Midden* (children's verse in Scots).

Carla Jetko is a Canadian living in the Hebrides. Her work is richly textured with a hedonistic edge which reflects her other career as a chef. Publishing credits include *Orbis Quarterly Journal*, *Edinburgh Review,* and *Poetry Scotland*. Carla's first poetry collection *The Body Banquet* explores obsession with food and the self.

Allan Knox was born in Edinburgh in 1968. Educated in Dalkeith at Langlaw Primary, Newbattle High School and Jewel & Esk Valley College. Ex-civil servant. Failed musician and songwriter. First attempts at poetry (including 'Shell Suits') written while studying a creative writing course at Newbattle Abbey College of Adult Education in 2002. Currently studying history and philosophy at Edinburgh University.

Norman Kreitman, retired Edinburgh psychiatrist, has written on the philosophy of language (*The Roots of Metaphor*, 1999) and has published two books of poetry (*Toughing Rock* and *Against Leviathan*). His third collection of verse, *Casanova's 72nd Birthday*, will appear early in 2004.

Helen Lamb is an award winning short-story writer and poet. Her short-story collection, *Superior Bedsits*, was published by Polygon, 2001. A poetry collection, *Strange Fish*, appeared in 1997. Her work has also been widely published in anthologies and magazines and broadcast on Radio 4, Radio Scotland and RTE. She was awarded SAC writing bursaries in 1999 and 2002, and is currently the Royal Literary Fund fellow at Edinburgh University's Office of Lifelong Learning.

Douglas Lipton's life has been spent in Glasgow and Dumfriesshire. Publications include: *The Stone Sleeping-Bag* (Mariscat), three chapbook selections (Markings Press) and an edition of poetry by children, *Chinese Spare-Ribs*. Recently, he has been writing a novel and a putative biography of the 18th century poet, Jenny Graham.

Christine De Luca has had three collections in English and Shetlandic published (*Voes & Sounds* (1994), *Wast wi da Valkyries* (1997) and *Plain Song* (2002)) and several commissions. She has worked with translators, artists and musicians and is one of the Shore Poets. Readings have taken her to Helsinki and Milan.

Lynda McDonald grew up in Grimsby, taught in Tower Hamlets, East London; but has lived longest in Edinburgh. She has published short stories, including one in *SHORTS* (Polygon). Reads prolifically and is currently enjoying the M.Phil Creative Writing course at Glasgow University.

Stuart Robert Macdonald was brought up in rural south-west Scotland but has lived in and travelled to many places. He presently lives in Edinburgh working as a data librarian at the university. He has had poems published in numerous publications in the last two years and is currently working on a first collection.

Ian McDonough was born in Brora, Sutherland, and works as a mediator in Edinburgh. His first volume of poetry, *Clan MacHine*, published by Chapman last year, was shortlisted for the Saltire Scottish First Book Award. His play *51 Pegasus* toured Scotland in 2002. He is Convenor of Edinburgh's Shore Poets.

James McGonigal (b.1947) is a teacher and editor whose poetry has won awards in Scotland and Ireland. His long poem *Passage/An Pasáiste* will be published by Mariscat Press in 2004.

Mary McIntosh: ex jute weaver turned teacher, now retired, lives in Kirriemuir. Writes mainly in Scots. Published in *Lallans, Chapman, NorthWords and Riverrun,* also various anthologies including *A Tongue in Yer Heid* and *Weavers Tales.* Writes short plays for local Community Drama groups and recently began writing poetry.

Màrtainn Mac ant-Saoir (Martin MacIntyre) was brought up in Lenzie, Glasgow with South Uist family connections. He has been writing poetry and prose in Gaelic and English for a number of years. *Ath-Aithne (Re-acquaintance)*, his first collection of Gaelic and English short stories (CLÀR, Ùr-Sgeul series), won the Saltire First Book Award in 2003. He recently completed a collection of Gaelic and English poems and is currently working on a Gaelic novel.

David Mackenzie comes from Easter Ross. His stories have been published in *Stand Magazine*, *Edinburgh Review*, *Chapman* and *New Writing Scotland* 20. His first novel, *The Truth of Stone* (Mainstream, 1991) was shortlisted for the Saltire Best Scottish First Book award.

Born in England of Irish parents, **Olivia McMahon** has lived in Aberdeen for the last 35 years. Her poetry has been widely published in magazines and she is currently putting a collection together. She is also finishing her second novel.

Iain S. MacPherson was born on the Canadian prairie, with family from Prince Edward Island. After university, he taught French Immersion high school before coming to Scotland. He currently lectures in Gaelic at Sabhal Mòr Ostaig, and comments on the Middle-East for BBC Gaelic.

Michael Malone is an Ayrshire man and has been widely published in the literary press. He was the Scottish Correspondent for *Writers Forum*. His first crime novel won the Pitlochry Prize from the Scottish Association of Writers and he acts as Trustee for the Petra Kenney Literature Foundation.

Andy Manders is from Highland Perthshire. Poet, educator and dad, his work appears in publications (including *NWS* 17, 18 & 20) and landscapes across Scotland. *wee girl* and *bairnie sang* come courtesy of a girl called Finn.

Lyn Moir was born in Scotland, educated there and in the USA, and lived in Southampton for 38 years. Since her return to Scotland, she has published two collections, *Me and Galileo* (pamphlet, 2001) and *Breakers' Yard* (2003) (both Arrowhead Press). She lives on the harbour in St Andrews.

Michael Munro, born Glasgow 1954, works as a freelance editor and lexicographer. Poems and stories in various anthologies and magazines. Author of *The Patter* (Glasgow Libraries, 1985), *The Complete Patter* (Birlinn, 2001), and *The Crack* (Birlinn, 2002).

Anne B. Murray was born in Glasgow where she now lives, writes and works as a creative writing tutor with groups of carers, and facilitates writing workshops and poetry readings for other community groups. She has had poetry published by Survivors' Poetry Scotland, in *Cutting Teeth* and in various anthologies.

Donald S. Murray is from Ness, Isle of Lewis and now lives and works as a teacher in Benbecula. His short story collection *Special Deliverance* (Scottish Cultural Press) was shortlisted for a Saltire Award and his poetry has been widely published – including *West Coasters*, a pamphlet based on his journeys to various islands, including Cape Clear and the three Aran islands.

Tracy Patrick is editor of *Earth Love*, a new small press nature-themed poetry magazine, featuring new and established writers, that donates all proceeds to environmental causes. She also performs spoken word, has won poetry slams in Glasgow and Edinburgh and has had poetry published in various magazines and anthologies.

Olive M. Ritch moved from Orkney to Aberdeen several years ago and is now studying English at the University of Aberdeen. She has poems published in several anthologies and literary magazines. She is currently working on her first collection.

Lesley Sargent was born in Edinburgh in 1965, but has spent the last eight years living in the south of Ireland. Her work attempts to reveal that which would otherwise remain unnoticed, focussing especially on elements of nature which humankind is becoming increasingly distant from.

Andrew Murray Scott's début novel *Tumulus* won the inaugural Dundee Book Prize in 1999 and was followed in 2001 by *Estuary Blue*. His twelve non-fiction book titles include an influential biography of Alex Trocchi, *The Making of the*

Monster and a two-volume guide, *Dundee's Literary Lives*. Website: **www.andrewmurrayscott.com.**

Frances Sessford was shortlisted for the 2002 *Scotland on Sunday*/Macallan prize and had two stories published in the ensuing *Macallan Shorts 5* anthology. She works full-time as an editor, lives in Perthshire and is involved in a race against impending motherhood to finish her first novel before February.

Morelle Smith's most recent poetry collection is *Deepwater Terminal* (diehard). Her poetry and fiction have appeared in magazines and anthologies, in collaborative exhibitions with visual artists, on the Glasgow Underground and on LRT buses. *Epirus Nights* (poetry) and *The Bridge on Sami Frasheri* (short stories) will be published in 2004.

Yvonne Spence has been published in several publications including *NWS 14,* and was a prizewinner in the *She* 1997 short story competition. In 2001 she graduated in Creative Writing from University College Chichester. Born in Shetland, she lives in Edinburgh with her family and is working on a novel.

Gary Steven grew up in the Southside of Glasgow, went to school there and then to Glasgow University where he studied English Literature and Philosophy before doing the MPhil in Creative Writing.

Mike Stocks lives in Edinburgh. His poems and translations have appeared in magazines such as *Chapman, The Dark Horse, Acumen, Outposts, Magma* and *Staple.* His children's books were recently re-published here and in the US. He is the editor of *Anon*, a poetry magazine that uses anonymous sub-mission procedures (**www.blanko.org.uk/anon**).

Alison Swinfen was born and brought up in Sheffield, did a degree in French and German at the University of Durham and a PhD at the University of Sheffield. She lives and works in Glasgow and is a member of the Iona Community.

Judith Taylor was born and brought up in Perthshire. A librarian by profession, she lived in Fife for some time but has recently moved to Aberdeen. She began writing poetry after she stopped studying it, and her work has appeared in a number of publications in Scotland and beyond.

Sheila Templeton was born in Aberdeen, then spent an itinerant childhood ranging from Rannoch Moor to Dar-es-Salaam. She has now settled by the sea in Ayrshire. Her poems have been published in *New Writing Scotland*, *Poetry Scotland* and *The Herald*. She won the SAW Poetry Trophy 2002, the local Ottakar's Poetry Competition 2003 and major awards in the Killie Writing Competition.

Fiona Ritchie Walker is from Montrose, now living in NE England. Her poetry has been published in magazines and anthologies, including the British Council's *New Writing 11*. Her first collection *Lip Reading* was published by Diamond Twig in 1999 and a second will be published by Iron Press in 2005.

Luke Williams was born in 1977. He's spent most of his life in Fife, but now lives in Norfolk. He studied history at Edinburgh University and Creative Writing at UEA. In 2003 he was the recipient of the Charles Pick Fellowship. *Questions, I* is the first chapter of a novel which will be published by Hamish Hamilton in 2007.

Jim C. Wilson lives in East Lothian. He has been widely published over the last 20 years, and has won several competitions (including the Scottish International Open). He was a Royal Literary Fund Writing Fellow (2001-2003), and has run Poetry in Practice groups at Edinburgh University since 1994.

Jonathan Wonham was born in Glasgow in 1965. He attended Gordonstoun School and the Universities of London and Liverpool. He has worked as a geologist in London, Aberdeen and Paris. His poetry has been published in *Poetry Introduction 7* (Faber, 1990) and a number of magazines.